A Journey with Panic

WITH the LATEST ADVICE on how to STOP PANIC SYMPTOMS using CBT

Written by Dr James Manning &
Dr Nicola Ridgeway

Published by the West Suffolk CBT Service
Angel Corner
8 Angel Hill
Bury St Edmunds
Suffolk
England

A Journey with Panic: With the latest advice on how to stop panic symptoms using CBT

Written by

Dr James Manning, ClinPsyD
Dr Nicola Ridgeway, ClinPsyD

Published by

The West Suffolk CBT Service Ltd, Angel Corner, 8 Angel Hill, Bury St Edmunds, Suffolk, IP33 1UZ

This edition printed 2016

Acknowledgements
We would like to thank Lorna for going through our original manuscript and copy-editing it. This has resulted in a large number of improvements to our original draft. Thanks also to Simon P. who helped a lot with several good ideas.

About the authors

Dr Nicola Ridgeway is a Consultant Clinical Psychologist and an accredited cognitive and behavioural therapist. She lectured on cognitive behaviour therapy (CBT) at the University of East Anglia, Suffolk, England, and the University of Essex for many years before becoming the Clinical Director of the West Suffolk CBT Service Ltd. Together with Dr James Manning she has co-authored several books on CBT.

Dr James Manning is a Consultant Clinical Psychologist and the Managing Director of the West Suffolk CBT Service. James has post-graduate qualifications in both Clinical Psychology and Counselling Psychology. He has regularly offered workshops and training to clinicians throughout the United Kingdom on Cognitive Behaviour Therapy and continues to work as a practicing therapist.

Also by Dr James Manning & Dr Nicola Ridgeway

Contents

Foreword by Dr James Manning

I suffered with mental health problems for many years before I got the help I needed, and in more stressful periods of my life, I experienced panic attacks from time-to-time. Fortunately, I found a way through my panic attacks by reading self-help books. Perhaps reading such books stimulated my interest in psychology, it's hard to say for sure. One thing I am grateful for is the freedom that psychological knowledge has given me. It has given me a life I value living and it has offered me an opportunity to help many others along the way.

At the risk of sounding a total f..k-up I'll tell you a bit about my life. Hopefully, it will give you some kind of an idea about how I developed such a passionate interest in psychology.

I have always had quite an obsessive personality and in my early teenage years I had quite a few problems with obsessive compulsive disorder. I knew that I was different from other people at a very young age, as did my family, but I didn't have any explanation for it. As I got older, I attempted to cope with problems that life presented me using food, drugs, gambling, and alcohol. I developed a significant alcohol problem as soon as I looked old enough to buy alcohol from an off-licence, (which was when I was about 16 or 17).

Between the ages of 15 and 30, I experienced a type of depression, known as dysthymia. Before this, I experienced sensory hyper-sensitivity, excessive avoidance, attention deficit, significant obsessive problems, paranoia, and anxiety.

In my late teenage years the emotion that affected me the most was low mood - I had a feeling of being slowed down, and an emptiness that sapped my motivation to engage in life. Normal events seemed more effortful and I found myself withdrawing from day-to-day activities. I started to feel unsettled most of the time, waking up early for no apparent reason - often at 4.00am - churning thoughts over and over in my mind, and not being able to go back to sleep. I withdrew from people, preferring to be alone. I became snappy and irritable, and felt on edge. My relationships generally suffered, and I lost most of my friendships.

I didn't have a very eventful childhood, relatively speaking, at least not when compared to stories I have heard from many of my clients. I was bullied physically by older children and bullied emotionally by my peers (mainly for being socially backward), and I experienced some mild trauma. Both of my parents were working class people who performed well in their careers and rose through the ranks of their respective companies, in my father's case to a top management position. My father was a perfectionist and highly obsessive. His perfectionist nature paid huge dividends for him at work -

financially and professionally. He supervised award winning civil engineering work. I saw an old photograph of him recently, being given an award by the Queen of England. He had a tendency to be obsessive in all areas, including at home, and became angry at even slight violations of his high standards. Let's say as a hormonal teenager, I violated his standards pretty much all of the time and he struggled with parenting me as a teenager. In retrospect, he probably found me quite difficult to parent because he noticed things in me that he didn't like about himself.

Both my parents emigrated from Ireland when they were teenagers. They were very young when thrust into the responsibilities of parenthood and as you might expect from young parents, they didn't really have much experience of looking after children, but they were really no different from my friends' parents.

I think my parents did their best to bring me up, based on the knowledge they had, but I struggled with being a child. I can still hear my mother's voice saying the words she repeated almost daily in her soft Irish accent: "Childhood are the best years of your life, enjoy it while you can." This confused me as my childhood felt terrible! And, and to make matters worse it seemed like my life was going to go downhill even further if these were the best years of my life. I had low self-esteem, and deeply entrenched beliefs that I was inadequate, stupid, bad, defective, weak, weird, and worthless as a person. I had no one I could talk to so I kept my fears to myself and spent a a lot of my time fighting my beliefs, keeping them hidden while I worked to prove them wrong.

As a young person, there were a number of positives that I could have drawn something from. By the time I reached 15, outsiders would have considered me a privileged child. I had some friends, and I had the support of a well-off family. I lived in a leafy suburb just outside London, and I had gained entry to a state selective grammar school, which at the time was one of the top schools in the country.

Unfortunately, however, I was not able to use what I had been given. By the age of 15, depression had started to hit me quite hard and my motivation to engage in life began to drop significantly. School teachers were not impressed with my academic performance and reported back to my parents that I was under-achieving academically. I passed my first set of exams at 16 and went on to do advanced exams, where I achieved less than spectacular results. By the time I was doing my advanced exams, teachers had noticed the changes in my behaviour and had begun to monitor me more closely. One day my chemistry teacher approached me with a frown etched on his forehead - even more than usual - and muttered "If you're not paranoid you should be!" A short time later I was told that the teachers held a meeting about me and I was placed on report; this is where teachers monitor a student much more closely and have regular meetings with them. By then I had dropped out of most of my sports teams such as rugby and cross-

country, I struggled with my friendship groups and eventually found myself dropped from them. Things weren't really going too well from a teenager's point of view. By this time, I already felt that I was a failure in life.

After leaving school you could say that I had a lucky break and gained a position in a small commodity brokers. I struggled to retain this role, not because of my ability to do the technical part of the job, but because of my lack of ability to regulate my mood and deal with interpersonal conflict. Basically, I found it difficult to get on with people. One day I found myself challenging a commodity trader for breaking what I thought were the rules of trading. The problem was that he worked for a very important client. The next day I was invited to my Managing Director's office and given my notice.

A number of further jobs followed, assisted at times by the support of my parents, but again I experienced interpersonal problems and had further dismissals. As time progressed, I found that my CV was beginning to look less and less promising as I moved from one job to another. On paper I thought I had begun to look unemployable and out of desperation began working for financial companies with dubious or unethical outlooks. I took a job in London working for a company that I hadn't looked into too much. I soon discovered after reading letters from clients that the company had previously been a very sophisticated boiler house. I couldn't work for companies like this, due to my moral stance on life. Following this, I continued to work my way down the pay scale hierarchy. Eventually the only work I could find was temporary work in factories, delivering pizza, and working as a cleaner for a minimum wage. A friend of mine Jo, a fund manager at Hill Samuel (a leading Merchant bank in London at the time) tried to call me and left messages with my parents over a period of several months. I didn't return his calls. I treated him very poorly considering we had developed a close friendship over a number of years. I basically abandoned him with no thought about how it might affect him.

Moving from plush offices to factories and such was a bit of a culture shock for me and I was dismissed from two of my minimum wage cleaning jobs for not following the requested instructions. I am embarrassed to admit that practically the only job I didn't get the sack from before I was twenty-eight was my pizza delivery job at Pizza Hut, and even that job was painful sometimes. From time-to-time I found myself delivering pizza to some of my now successful Grammar School peers who appeared speechless when they opened their door to find me standing there with a pizza for them.

By that time my sense of inadequacy was fully reinforced and I had switched off emotionally. During this period of time I became quite hard-up financially and my mind set had become quite extreme and rigid. I didn't want to use the unemployment system or to ask my parents for help as in my mind this would have confirmed to me that I really was not succeeding in life. Sometimes I couldn't earn enough money to pay rent, so I ended up spending months living in a tent at a campsite where the rent was £4 per day. At other times I could pay the rent but was left eating potatoes and baked beans as my only source of nourishment.

I continuously felt that I was failing in some way. I felt empty inside. I just didn't feel like I had the energy to do things; I wanted to escape from my problems and myself. The only time I really felt OK was when I was asleep. I became quite avoidant and more nocturnal. I often did not attend events that I had been invited to, mostly without sending an apology or letting people know. I didn't answer the phone to friends or return their calls. The number of friends I had dwindled to just one. I think the only way that this friend managed to tolerate me was to laugh about the way I behaved, and to recognise that my behaviour was not about him. I felt so insignificant that I genuinely believed other people wouldn't notice or care whether I turned up late for planned events, or would even be bothered if I attended them at all. *All my focus was on myself.* It was a pitiful kind of self-loathing with endless self-questioning about why my life was so broken. I was so detached that I had little regard for other people's feelings or my own. Most of the time I did not want to live anymore and hoped I would die.* It was as if my body, mind, and my personality, were so unacceptable to me that I despised myself.

Luckily, in my very late twenties and early thirties I found a few excellent therapists. I worked hard on my therapy - which in my case needed a couple of years, as I had left things for so long before getting help. I brought negative and self-defeating thoughts that I had into conscious awareness and began to make significant changes to my life. I changed my life using many of the processes I have covered in this book. I'm 49 now, and I have been fortunate to have worked with Dr Nicola Ridgeway in treating several thousand clients over the years, and I haven't looked back since. I am still grateful to have the opportunity to help others who are stuck to move on with their lives.

I continue to use many of the exercises and coping strategies that I learnt in my therapy to keep in a good state of well-being. I can state categorically that if I were to stop using my coping strategies now, I would very quickly drift back into mental health problems. I have learnt that Cognitive Behaviour Therapy (CBT) is not a quick fix. Many people make initial positive gains after a completing a course of CBT, but most relapse after a number of years. This does not mean that CBT is not effective, as it works when people are using it. In reality, it means that people have stopped using the strategies that they worked on during their therapy. An important message that I would like to get across to you, therefore, is that CBT is delivered over a short time, <u>but it is not a short-term therapy</u>

*Except when I had panic attacks. I really didn't want to die when I had those.

How to use this book

I wrote this book because I found that many of my clients found it very difficult to remember topics discussed in their CBT sessions. I discovered that giving people hand-outs tended to help a bit, but that sheets of A4 paper tended to get lost quite easily. I wanted to find a way to help my clients to keep a permanent record of their progress, so that they could look back over what they did at any time in the future. The outcome is the book that you are reading right now.

Making records can be very helpful when you complete CBT. You can write notes in this book before, during, and after your sessions. This book can be used as a memory aid, and to complete homework tasks set by your therapist.

Many people don't like writing in books, and in most of the CBT books I've looked at the pages are a little too small to write in. So I've made this book especially large, just so you can write in it. So please write in it! Write all over it if you like. If you are having one-to-one CBT sessions take it with you to your sessions, and use it to make notes during, or after your meetings.

When you have CBT, your therapist might not always have the worksheets that you need, and sometimes the sheets that are given out can end up all over the place. This book will help you to keep your worksheets in one place, so that they don't get misplaced or lost. You can also use this book to complete homework tasks set by your therapist.

What is a panic attack?

I remember my first panic attack quite clearly. I was 22 years old and as you might understand the experience took me completely by surprise. I had just returned home from an ordinary evening at the pub, when all of a sudden I noticed my head felt incredibly light. My mind was spinning and I felt like I was drifting out of my body. All I could think was "This is the end!" "This is it!" I could hear the pounding of my heart as it began to thump like crazy in my chest and I rushed to the bathroom. I can't remember at the time why, but I thought the bathroom might help. I was leaning over the sink, splashing water over my head, as in this state I thought somehow that this might keep me alive.

Meanwhile, my concerned brother was following me about as I rushed from one place to another. He kept trying to talk to me, asking what was wrong with me, but I had no time to listen to his questions and I couldn't really hear what he was saying. All I can remember was feeling absolutely desperate. I recall telling my brother "I'm dying!" "I can't breathe!" Nothing I tried seemed to help. My fight with what I thought was the 'death process' seemed to go on for ages, probably about twenty minutes, until eventually, I tried watching the television and after half an hour the problem seemed to completely disappear... After that, I congratulated myself on my lucky escape and tried not to think about it anymore. I blocked the whole event from my mind and pretended it hadn't happened. When my brother brought it up a few days later, I told him that I didn't want to talk about it. The experience left me believing I was weak as a person for reacting that way. I felt ashamed and embarrassed.

If the above thoughts and feelings are familiar to you, then like me, you will truly know what it is like to feel haunted by panic attacks. I found that my fear of having further panic attacks tortured me and this fear didn't go away by itself.

Fortunately as time progressed, I read self-help books, and the main thing I discovered was that I was able to reduce my symptoms by understanding the **physiology of panic** – or what happens in the body when we panic. I suggest that you also find out how panic attacks work, because if you are able to understand what's happening to you, or if you can observe that you are having a panic attack rather than what you think is a life threatening event your distress will reduce significantly. After you have read about how panic attacks work, you can try some of the coping strategies that I will describe for you in the latter part of this book.

What is a panic attack?

Technically speaking a panic attack is a whole body response to perceived threat or danger. If you've had a panic attack you will know just how strong the bodily sensations are (see figure 1). You'll also be aware that one of the most confusing issues with panic

attacks is that they occur mostly when there's no real physical danger. After all, most people aren't worried about experiencing panic type symptoms when there's a good reason to panic, for example, if there's a fire.

What happens to the body during a panic attack?

Imagine we were lucky enough to be informed by a team of experts in a TV documentary describing what's happening to a young man in real time while he's in the process of having a panic attack.

The Radiologist

A Radiologist - doctor who interprets scans - is the first to speak in our documentary as she shows us a brain scan with a tiny almond shaped area shining brightly deep inside the man's brain. She explains that this is his amygdala firing up. (Dresler et al, 2011). As this light shines we're shown data spikes occurring in bio-feedback machines such as blood pressure monitors, electrocardiograms (ECG's) and other devices that are hooked up to the young man.

The Cardiologist

Next the documentary cuts to a Cardiologist - a medical expert in the heart. He explains that the man's heart rate and blood pressure are both increasing as his heart needs to pump large volumes of blood to his major muscle groups and to maintain blood-flow to these areas. He explains that this process enables the man's muscles to become oxygenated and to move very quickly if required. He tells us that the average man's body holds only 4.5 litres of blood and this blood cannot be everywhere at the same time. He says that as blood flow is maintained to the man's major muscle groups, it is diverted away from the parts of his body that aren't contributing to his panic response.

The Gastroenterologist

Our documentary now takes us to a Gastroenterologist (a medical expert in the gut and digestion) who explains that the digestive tract, bowel and bladder are particularly affected by panic symptoms (Logue et al, 2011). She says that this makes good logical sense as the man's body does not want to be processing food and waste material when it's in a state of threat. The Gastroenterologist shows us a scan of the man's stomach and digestive system contracting leading to a variety of unpleasant physical sensations in these areas of his body. We notice his stomach cramping, feelings of nausea etc. We witness his bladder and bowels being particularly affected as they want to shut up shop, leaving him with a feeling of wanting to visit the bathroom.

The Anaesthetist

Next to present is an Anaesthetist (a medical expert in anaesthetics) who happens to be monitoring the man's vital signs. He tells us that in line with the maintenance of blood flow required for the man's panic response, the man's body is increasing its blood pressure and consuming more oxygen. He says that the man is beginning to hyperventilate as he starts to breath out too much carbon dioxide. The Anaesthetist tells us that the man probably feels as though he can't breathe or that he is going to suffocate, but reassures us that he needs to do nothing as the young man is perfectly safe. The Anaesthetist tells us that the man's body is now heating up which means it will shortly need to activate its cooling system (i.e., induce sweating). He points to the man's body as it starts to tremble slightly (caused by rapid movement of blood around the man's body) and says that the man may feel hot in some parts and colder in others. The Anaesthetist tells us that multiple sensory areas are contained in the tips of the fingers and toes, and that the tips of fingers and toes do not need blood when faced with a survival threat. He tells us that blood is moved out of finger tips and toes leaving the man with a loss of feeling in these highly sensitive body areas.

The Clinical Psychologist

A Psychologist is the last expert to speak in our documentary. She invites us to look into the mind of the young man. She says that changes will be occurring in the man's brain affecting his sensory functioning. She tells us that he will probably have increased sensory perception in terms of what he is able to smell, see, and hear (Krusemark & Li, 2012). She says that due to the man's increase in auditory perception (hearing) he notices an increased awareness of his heart beat and he can clearly hear it pounding. The Psychologist asks him to complete some basic cognitive tasks and reports back her results. She suggests that the rational parts of the man's brain are beginning to become disrupted by his panic response. She says that as a result of this it is now very difficult for him to plan, think clearly, or make informed decisions. (I will explain why this occurs in chapter 3.) She tells us that he is now likely to enter into a primitive, **default-type** response, which basically means that he is somewhat compelled to behave automatically, without thinking. She says that means that he is likely to use the same way of coping with panic over and over again.

Looking for meaning

When the above types of bodily processes occur to you for the first time, you will be unfamiliar with what is happening and you may become very frightened and look inwards. I'd like you to bear in mind that it is completely natural to look to understand why you are having such an experience. Common thoughts fed back from your mind to create meaning might be "I am going to have a heart attack," "I am going to lose control", "I'm going insane", "I am going to die", "I'm having a stroke", "I'm going to lose control of my bladder", and "There is something terribly wrong with me."

I imagine that after you had your first panic attack, like me, you were probably wondering "Why am I suffering with these symptoms, while everybody else seems to be getting on with their lives?"

Who suffers with panic attacks?

Many more people suffer with panic attacks than you might know about. As a therapist I have offered treatment to several thousand people. Many people feel ashamed of their symptoms and like I did, don't openly discuss their problems even with their closest friends or relatives. The truth of the matter is that panic experiences are human and affect people in all walks of life. There are no boundaries to who can suffer from panic and sufferers range from the intellectually gifted (e.g., Sir Isaac Newton, Sigmund Freud), to national leaders (e.g., Sir Winston Churchill, Abraham Lincoln).

Coping with panic?

Each of us has our own instinctive coping strategies for reacting to our panic sensations. In my clinical practice I have witnessed a range of responses. Some people become very quiet when they are having a panic attack. A natural safety mechanism is to restrict movement, a bit like small insects do when there is a chance that they may become a meal for a nearby predator. On the other hand, I have also seen people who flail around grabbing furniture, and at the time are unable to have concern for others thoughts about them - especially if they believe they are about to die!

Figure 1. What happens in the body when we panic

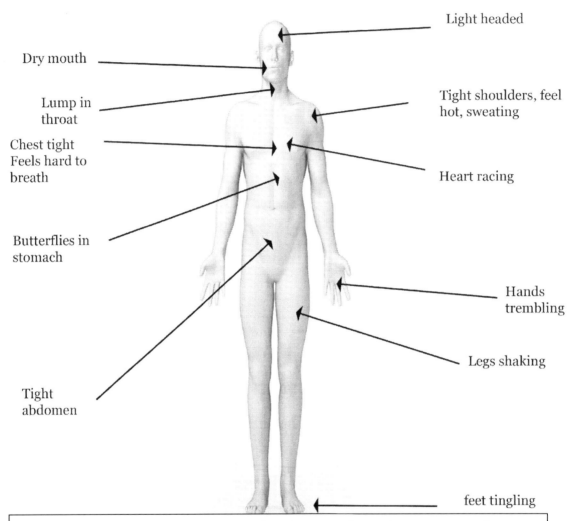

Light headed

Dry mouth

Lump in throat

Tight shoulders, feel hot, sweating

Chest tight Feels hard to breath

Heart racing

Butterflies in stomach

Hands trembling

Legs shaking

Tight abdomen

feet tingling

Research - In 2012 Elizabeth Krusemark and Wen Li from the University of Wisconsin used functional magnetic resonance imagery (a brain scan) to assess the impact of anxiety on smell. They found that when people became more anxious their sense of smell became enhanced. In a separate study completed by Malizia and colleagues in 1998, positron emission tomography - another type of brain scan - was used to look specifically at the amygdala when people were anxious. They found that those individuals suffering with panic attacks had 'defective' inhibition of their amygdala. In essence, people suffering with panic attacks had less ability to over-ride their natural threat based response.

Chapter summary

What is a panic attack?

- Panic attacks generally occur in the absence of any real physical threat.

- The body develops a panic response after receiving messages from the amygdala.

- Significant physical changes occur very quickly, these include rapid heartbeat, contraction of the digestive system, sweating, bodily trembling, breathing changes, and difficulties thinking clearly.

- Panic attacks are very frightening and affect people from all walks of life.

- It is common to have frightening thoughts during a panic attack, as the human mind attempts to make sense of the whole experience.

- People who experience panic attacks have their own individual ways of coping and will often use the same behaviours over and over again automatically.

2 What makes a panic attack happen in the first place?

After you had your first panic attack you may well have asked yourself - "Why now? I wasn't doing anything out of the ordinary. It just doesn't make any sense!" You may also have spent some time worrying about your experience before getting any additional information or professional advice.

Many people who come to my clinic in Bury St Edmunds, Suffolk have already experienced panic attacks for quite a while before they visit me for an assessment. Generally, they will have built up their own coping strategies for dealing with their panic symptoms, with the most common approach being avoidance of situations that trigger panic. Unfortunately, however, my clients generally find that avoiding panic symptoms often makes their problems worse and their lives become even more restricted. From my point of view as their therapist it is hard work - but not impossible - to break down their avoidant strategies, especially if they have become habitual after years of use. If you have experienced panic attacks for a long time, I will explain how you can break these habit patterns later in the book. However, before you skip there right now I urge you to look at the real causes of your first panic attack as understanding the processes that led to it will be invaluable.

Stress and panic attacks

As I mentioned at the beginning of this chapter a question that people carry in their minds after having a panic attack is **"Why now?"** and **"What was that?"**

Figure 2 shows an imaginary graph of how anxiety/stress levels may fluctuate over time. It is important to note that many individuals who experience panic attacks are not used to noticing how tense they feel. As a result their stress and anxiety levels can build up to quite high levels without them necessarily being aware of it (Grant & Kinman, 2010).

My thoughts on panic based on clinical experience

I would like you to imagine that there is panic attack critical zone. This critical zone represents the point your body needs to cross before it goes into panic (see figure 3.) If you hover just below this critical zone you will be unaware that you are just a hairs breath away from experiencing panic. In this respect only a very small additional stressor, (i.e., the straw that breaks the camel's back) could send you over the tipping point into panic (see figure 3.)

Often a panic attack will occur in a situation that you have been in several times before without any difficulties. Examples might be while driving, while a passenger on a plane, tube, or taxi, while at a social event, after a normal day at work, while out shopping, when going to bed, while withdrawing from alcohol, or even while watching the TV.

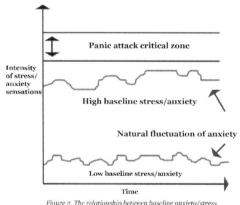

Figure 2. The relationship between baseline anxiety/stress levels and vulnerability to a panic attack over time.

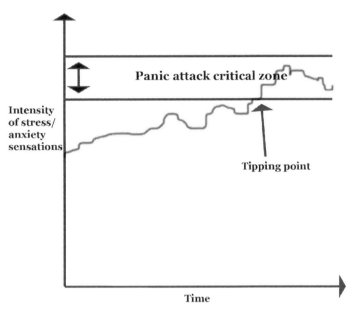

Figure 3. Development of first panic attack

Research

In 2012 Brazilian researchers Ruan Cabral and Antonio Nardi screened and reviewed 11 major studies on anxiety and panic attacks. They found that all the studies they selected for investigation pointed towards a 'facilitating and non-inhibitory effect of anxiety on panic attacks'. In other words feeling anxious was necessary to create an environment for panic attacks to occur.

Research

In 2010 Gail Kinman and Louise Grant completed a study with 240 trainee social workers, an occupation in which the work is notorious for high degrees of stress and burn out. Amongst their many findings they found that social workers with lower scores for a) emotional intelligence and b) reflective abilities were less resilient and more emotionally distressed. A simple conclusion drawn by Kinman & Grant was that if social worker trainees were encouraged to work on abilities such as a) reflection and b) emotional understanding they would become more resilient in the workplace.

Chapter summary

What makes a panic attack happen in the first place?

- High overall stress and anxiety levels will increase your risk of experiencing a panic attack.

- Ironically, your first panic attack is most likely to occur in a situation that you have experienced several times before without any difficulty.

The structure of the brain

In this chapter I am going to explain how the brain's alarm system works by simplifying a highly complex neuro-biological process.

The brain

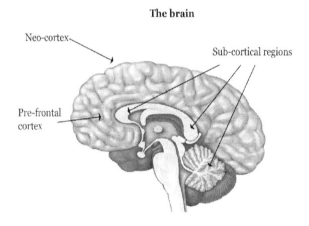

Figure 4. Structure of the brain

There are three main structures that it is advisable to know about to understand panic. These areas are the neo-cortex, the pre-frontal cortex, and the sub-cortical regions, see figure 4.

Neo-cortex

This is a part of the brain responsible for thinking, planning, and logical thought. We use this part of the brain to understand language, to make calculations, and to problem-solve. This part of the brain is used quite a lot when we carry out complex thinking.

Pre-frontal cortex

The pre-frontal cortex is an essential part of the brain for psychological wellness. The pre-frontal cortex's main job is to act as a communication system between the neo-cortex and the sub-cortical region. It has many important functions. It quietens down noise in the mind and it can call off emotional reactions. We also use this part of our brain to think about our thinking and to bring choices into conscious awareness. The pre-frontal cortex becomes affected in people who experience panic symptoms and this can often leave individuals who panic feeling that they are unable to think straight.

The sub-cortical regions

The sub-cortical regions - which take their name because they are located underneath the brains outer cortex area - could be described as a primitive or animal brain, as we share similar brain structures with mammals. The sub-cortical regions' predominant interest is survival. This is where our main pleasure and pain centres are located.

Sub-cortical regions of the brain become highly active when we experience perceived threat; whether real or imagined. When people become highly anxious sub-cortical brain regions release neurochemicals known as **catecholamines** which improve the way that primitive brain regions function. In lay terms, catecholamines work a bit like a turbo-boost or a power-up for the animal brain. When primitive brain regions become more active, people become more aware of all of their senses. As a result of this, they may see, hear, feel, taste, and smell things more strongly (Guzman, Tronson, Jovasevic Sato, Guedea, Mizukami, Nishimori & Radulovic, 2013). This process is not without problems, however. Catecholamines although enhancing the effects of the sub-cortical region leach or spread into the nearby pre-frontal cortex and stop it functioning effectively. This leaching effect is usually only temporary and when the threat dies down and neurochemicals are reabsorbed, the pre-frontal cortex starts to work normally as before.

Examples of how different parts of the brain communicate in real life.

The brains internal communication system won't make much sense unless we examine how it functions in day-to-day existence, so I will draw on some examples from my life. Historically, I have had some difficulties with ice cream. Unfortunately, the ice cream that I like tends to be the expensive type that comes in 500ml tubs with about 1300 calories in. My sub-cortical region experiences intense pleasure while eating these ice creams from beginning to end, and I have tended to use them as a reward over the years, which is not to be advised. After getting into a pattern of eating ice-cream for a period of time, I notice that my clothes are starting to feel a bit tight. My neo-cortex or logical mind comes on line and tells me that I am on a path to obesity, possible ill health, difficulties with my pancreas, and heart disease. I look in the mirror and I appear a bit bloated.

My partner gently mentions that I may be putting on a little bit of weight, <u>but tells me she still loves me</u>. I don't want to buy a whole new set of clothes. I recognise that I need to stop eating so much ice cream. Luckily, to assist me with my sense of internal conflict, I can engage my pre-frontal cortex much more to try to correct my habit and bring it into awareness - In essence, I use my pre-frontal cortex to make more conscious choices. For example, if I am in a supermarket and I feel an urge to buy ice-cream, I acknowledge these sensations and then direct my attention to something else instead; perhaps a really interesting book that I am going to read later, or a healthy snack, and I use these things as a replacement reward system.

Equally, if a new attractive staff member joins my office my sub-cortical region becomes highly stimulated - I recognise that I am an animal after all. My neo-cortex has a very different idea about a way ahead compared to my sub-cortical region; I have a great family and things are pretty good in my family life. I am faced with a slight conflict. Luckily, my pre-frontal cortex, comes on-line to assist me with my choices. If I am faced with a slight boundary issue or anything that might take me over a fine line in a relationship, I bring it to my awareness, make choices, and put new boundaries around the relationship to limit it developing any further. My neo-cortex, assisted by my pre-frontal cortex helps to suppress the impulses or urges that I feel, (which often pass very rapidly), and I am able to sustain my happy family existence.

What happens when we experience prolonged threat?

If we experience threat for prolonged periods the continuous release of catecholamines by sub-cortical regions, can gradually damage - or cause atrophy to - the pre-frontal cortex located right next to it, (Arnsten, Raskind, Taylor & Connor, 2015). (This generally results in the pre-frontal cortex working much less effectively.) When the pre-frontal cortex goes off line or begins to work less effectively we lose our ability to calm ourselves and we can begin to feel more agitated about things that we weren't really bothered about before. This occurs as the pre-frontal cortex can no longer supress emotional reactions triggered by sub-cortical regions. The neo-cortex (thinking/analytical brain) is also unable to function effectively as it relies heavily on the pre-frontal cortex to make decisions and direct attentional resources. This is generally why therapists suggest to their clients that they shouldn't make any important life decisions until they have recovered from their mental health problems. I have placed a link below to video which shows how this process works.

http://www.z1b6.com/4.html

So, in summary of this section, when people experience panic it is difficult for them to think straight and their minds feel foggy. The neo-cortex is not able to function properly as to do this it needs the assistance of the pre-frontal cortex to hold ideas in mind, and to think about thoughts at the at the same time. When the pre-frontal cortex comes back on line again people tend to find that they are able to think clearly once more.

Chapter summary

The structure of the brain

- The functioning of the brain can be separated into three main areas, the sub-cortical region, the pre-frontal cortex, and the neo-cortex.

- The sub-cortical region takes care of our animal functions, the neo-cortex deals with our complex thinking, and the pre-frontal cortex operates as a go between.

- The sub-cortical region becomes more dominant when we experience threat. The neo-cortex becomes more dominant when we are relaxed.

- If we experience threat for prolonged periods the pre-frontal cortex becomes less able to do its job effectively. This is when many of us may begin to struggle with mental health problems.

The brain's alarm system

In the middle of the sub-cortical regions of the brain lie our two amygdalae, see figure 5.

The brain

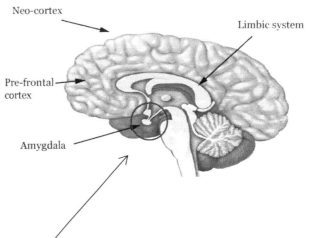

Figure 5. The location of the amygdala

The Threat Perception Centre

Research indicates that despite the small size of the amygdalae and the regions that surround it, this area of the brain has its own dedicated memory system which holds key information about past traumatic incidents (LeDoux, 2015). This memory system appears to operate like a lookout post or a sieve. It observes everything that passes through our senses and activates the amygdala if it notices any sensory stimuli that might be a slight match for past painful physical or psychological experiences. For simplicity I will refer to this memory system as the **'Threat Perception Centre.'**

I will illustrate how this process works with an example from my childhood. When I was around eight or nine I used to pick wild brambles and spent many hours enjoying myself looking for the largest ripest berries to eat. One summer day I picked what I thought was the ultimate bramble and was just about to put it in my mouth when I became aware of a maggot wriggling in the stem and touching my lips. I immediately felt a wave of disgust ripple through my whole body. I felt like practically every hair on my body stood on end as I immediately realised I could have eaten this maggot as well as others unknowingly. I instinctively threw the berry as far as I could away from me, then turned around and walked off.

After the above incident I developed an aversion to eating brambles, which progressed to supermarket berries, such as raspberries which had a similar shape, and then later to jams containing raspberries or blackberries. My body produced an automatic response to the cue of any fruit that was shaped anything like a blackberry. As a child I didn't stop to think about what was going on or to challenge my fears, I simply avoided eating these types of berries. I didn't view it as a problem and to be honest it didn't affect my life very much.

My situation with berries is typical of processes that occur in the sub-cortical region of the brain. According to models of emotional intelligence (Golman, 1997) the sub-cortical region, due to its more primitive nature puts a significant focus on

survival. It also obtains access to information from the senses slightly before the neocortex. If while accessing sensory information it picks up cues associated with past painful or frightening events (trauma) it immediately triggers biological processes that generate defensive or offensive type reactions (i.e., the fight-flight response). Importantly, it will also do this before the rational mind has a chance to think about what action to take. I have drawn a hypothetical, simplified model of how this process occurs (see figure 6).

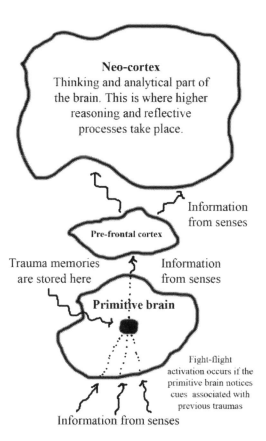

Figure 6. Model of the threat perception centre in action

At this point I am not going to go into great detail about the biology of the threat perception centre. If you are interested in finding out more about the biology of emotions you can find an excellent and highly readable review of this area within Daniel Goleman's book on Emotional Intelligence (1995). Early chapters in Goleman's book cover "Emotional Hijacking" whereas other areas within his book will help you understand how emotions work.

When the sub-cortical mind is helpful

Most of us, if we think about it enough, will probably be able to remember situations where our sub-cortical mind has helped ourselves or others in tricky situations. Indeed, while I was thinking of ideas for this book I remembered a potentially life changing incident that I observed one hot summer weekend in Suffolk, England. My family had been invited to a barbeque at a friend's house. Many friends and colleagues had brought their children. The children were playing in the garden and the adults were caught up in conversation around the host's outdoor pool. At one point I heard one lady whisper "Has anybody seen Molly?" Immediately out of the corner of my eye I noticed a heavily pregnant colleague of mine jumping fully clothed into the pool and a second or so later pulling a two year old girl out of the pool **by her hair**. The incident happened in seconds, and the whole rescue operation occurred before the rest of us had time to think (or to

activate our amygdalae). Molly's mother was in a state of shock when Molly was handed to her dazed but otherwise completely fine. I asked my therapist friend what had happened and she said that she didn't think about what she was doing, she just found herself jumping into the pool.

In a similar vein I can recall one personal incident were I instinctively picked up a two year old child (who was unknown to me) as he was about to walk in front of a fast moving vehicle. His mother was immensely grateful, but the truth of the matter was that I didn't really exercise a conscious choice over what I was doing. My arms reached out and picked up the child before I had a chance to think.

So in essence, following on from the above, the sub-cortical or primitive brain puts the body into a position where it can make physical decisions instantly. As you might imagine taking extra time to think about what to do in dangerous circumstances could mean the loss of vital seconds that literally make a difference between life and death.

When the sub-cortical mind is not helpful

Without doubt the sub-cortical region can literally be a life saver, but as you will be aware by now its life-saving function can also fire up when it's not actually needed - not unlike a highly sensitive fire alarm going off at the steam from your kettle. To understand this 'misfiring' I want to bring your attention back to the idea that the sub-cortical region has its own separate memory system for painful or frightening events from your past. Based on this, if your past panic attack was perceived as **traumatic** – which means that it was not fully processed or dealt with at an emotional level - a memory trace can remain in the threat perception centre's memory database (much as my bramble fruit experience was for me). The threat perception centre may then screen your body for potential cues associated with panic attacks such as light-headedness, raised heart rate, breathlessness, dizziness, etc. If these cues are noticed it will instigate a prepared state response, (see figure 7.) This is likely to mean more frequent experiences of anxiety together with an increase in sensitivity and **hypervigilance** - or being on the lookout - for perceived threat in your body. This process is likely to encourage you to remain alert to potential anxiety cues and results in your anxiety remaining high.

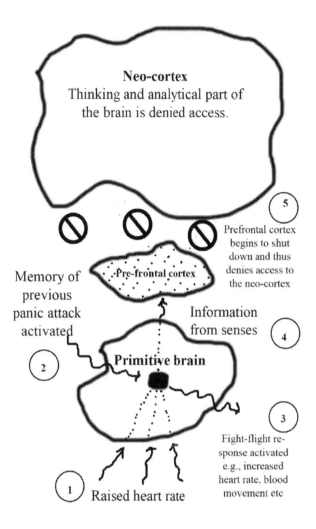

Figure 7. Raised heart rate and prepared response

Research

In 2015 academics Amy Armsten, Murray Raskind & their colleagues completed a review of clinical research looking into the impact of stress on the pre-frontal cortex. They found that a large number of studies clearly demonstrated that chronic stress led to a) marked impairment of the pre-frontal cortex as a result of catecholamine release and b) growth of the amygdala at a neurobiological level. In essence their investigation appeared to demonstrate that the longer an individual was exposed to chronic stress the less able they were to supress their natural fight-flight response, and the more active their threat response became.

Chapter summary

The brain's alarm system

- The sub-cortical region of the brain helps the body to take immediate action in the face of perceived threat.

- When working effectively the sub-cortical region can literally be a life saver.

- The threat perception centre records traumatic incidents in its memory to warn the individual against future similar dangers.

- An experience of a panic attack can be recorded as a traumatic incident resulting in an increase in sensitivity and vigilance to anxiety. This results in higher levels of stress and anxiety which can increase the probability of further panic attacks.

How are panic attacks kept in place?

One evening I was sitting on the family sofa, watching a world championship boxing match on TV, (in the days when you could watch it for free). As I got more engrossed in the match, I became aware that my heart was beating rapidly. This frightened me as I didn't understand how this could happen. I thought to myself "How can my heart be working so hard when I'm sitting down doing nothing?" All I felt I could do was to concentrate on my heart a bit more, hoping that it would slow down a bit. However, it seemed the more I concentrated on my heart, the worse it got and after a few minutes it was thumping like crazy. I started to become concerned that if it carried on beating at that rate I would end up having a heart attack so I got up and started pacing around the sitting room with my hand clasping my chest. In the end, I felt the only solution was to turn off the TV as I thought that this had triggered it. After a few minutes my heart started to slow down, and I began to feel relieved that I had a lucky escape.

The maintenance trio

In the previous three chapters, I offered you information about what a panic attack is and what brings it on in the first place. In the next three chapters I want us to look in more detail at a) what factors maintain symptoms of panic and b) the different types of behaviour that people carry out to cope with their fear of further panic attacks.

Thinking about the many clients I have treated for their panic attacks, there are three main ways they seem to react to their symptoms. These are

- Thinking "What is happening to me...?" The brain then launches into a list of catastrophic ideas (e.g., "This is dangerous!"). Changes in the body (e.g., raised heart rate) are then used as evidence to support catastrophic misinterpretations, for example, "I'm having a heart attack!" Alternatively clients may reassure themselves about their symptoms in a self-critical way, for example, "This is ridiculous!" "Come on get a grip!" "You're fine...everything is OK...you're just being silly!"
- Threat monitoring – continuously monitoring the body for signs of change, such as a raised heart rate and changes in breathing.
- Behavioural avoidance and safety behaviours – For example, avoiding situations that may be associated with panic, running through mental escape routes, sitting near the isle in a cinema, avoiding physical exertion, avoiding certain foods, only driving certain routes in a car, asking others for reassurance and such like.

A further problem tends to occur if the above strategies are used on a regular basis over a period of years. When offering therapy I have noticed that it takes a greater number of sessions for clients to recover, if they have developed habits associated with the maintenance trio. Sometimes I may need to help clients take apart years of subtle avoidance behaviours. (Later in this book I will show you how you can achieve this on your own or with help from a therapist.) On the other hand, when patterns of safety behaviours are less developed, recovery from experiencing panic attacks can occur more rapidly (in just one or two visits). In the following chapters I will focus on the individual elements of worry, threat monitoring, and behavioural avoidance one-by-one.

Chapter summary

How are panic attacks kept in place?

- Intuitively doing things to help yourself with panic symptoms can sometimes make the problem worse in the long-term.

- There are three main ways that people intuitively react to symptoms of panic. These are a) creating catastrophic thoughts through worry or attempting to reassure themselves, b) threat monitoring (vigilant checking for 'suspect' bodily sensations), behavioural avoidance, and c) safety behaviours.

Worry, and panic

"I recommend you spend less time in your cubicle."

When the pre-frontal cortex becomes unwell due to prolonged stress, we begin to worry more about things that we would not normally have been bothered about before. When this happens the pre-frontal cortex becomes less able to quieten down noise in the mind, and more frightening thoughts reach awareness. People become stuck in a worry loop (see figure 8) as they attempt to find solutions to cope with feared situations or outcomes that are actually generated by their own worry process. This activates the sub-cortical regions threat responses even more and reduces the input of the neo-cortex still further.

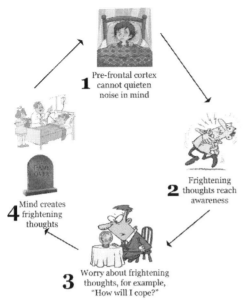

1 Pre-frontal cortex cannot quieten noise in mind

2 Frightening thoughts reach awareness

3 Worry about frightening thoughts, for example, "How will I cope?"

4 Mind creates frightening thoughts

Figure 8. worry loop

Why we worry

When we become anxious in response to what we consider to be usually non-threatening environmental triggers, such as driving a car on a motorway, a tendency for the majority of us as intelligent human beings is to search for meaning. As no communication about meaning is offered by the sub-cortical region it is intuitive for many of us to engage our higher brain functions to search for a rational explanation. This process involves asking questions generally preceded with the words "Why, what if, and how is it?"

Don't beat yourself up for worrying – It's completely natural

I look back on my undergraduate days as one of the most stimulating periods of my life. I recall undergraduate developmental psychology lecturers explaining that from infancy each of us has an inbuilt tendency to search for understanding about how and why the world operates around us the way it does. This is based on an idea that the more that we think we know the safer we feel. Lecturers in para-psychology informed us that when humans cannot explain why unknown processes occur they tend to make hypotheses, or to fill gaps in their knowledge using their imagination. They said that in the 15th Century unknown processes may have been referred to as magic, and people of that time may have carried out superstitious behaviours to protect themselves from things that they didn't understand.

Taking the above notions further, lecturers in evolutionary psychology told us that our search for answers was linked to our survival. They suggested that humans had very frail bodies, compared with other animals, and that it was our ability to think ahead and make predictions that helped humans survive. Indeed, they said that it is was our human vulnerability itself that probably forced our higher thinking abilities to develop more rapidly, leading to humans currently dominating the Earth's surface.

When our search for meaning makes us feel more anxious

I guess what I'm really getting at is that we are creatures that search for meaning. When we "Know' or "We think we know" we tend to relax a little, even when "What we know" isn't good news! States of perceived uncertainty or not knowing can be highly stressful for humans and when this occurs we try to reduce our distress by searching for meaning. This search for meaning can create a difficulty however. Problems are created when we use our higher brain functions or imagination to search for answers to an experience of anxiety or panic that we don't fully understand. Generally, if you ask your mind a question it will feel compelled to answer, even when it doesn't have accurate information available. It will often trawl through its database drip-feeding a variety of inaccurate ideas, thoughts, and images into conscious awareness.

Based on the above, if you use your mind to ask yourself "Why is my heart beating so fast?", "Why is my head spinning?", "Why aren't these feelings going away?" it will access what it has available. The human mind may not have any information about the bodily sensations associated with panic but it may have a lot of information - often inaccurate - about heart attacks, strokes, or psychiatric wards, and thus may put some of the following ideas forward as suggestions.

"It's probably nothing."

"You're having a heart attack."

"You're having a stroke."

"You're going to faint or blackout."

"I'm going to lose control of my body."

"You're going insane."

"You're going to die."

"I'm going to wet myself."

"I'm going to be sick."

As well as the aforementioned verbal based thoughts, the mind gives us information in many different formats from meaning-based thoughts to highly vivid images of what we think is happening and what we think is about to happen.

Highly frightening thoughts produced by the brain - **catastrophic thoughts** - are understandably accompanied by high levels of emotional distress as the amygdala (activated by catastrophic thoughts) increases the body's threat response still further. In this respect, higher levels of fear that accompany our anxiety-based thoughts and images increase the intensity of physical sensations even more. For example, feeling dizzy can progress to feeling disorientated. These experiences of heightened sensations may then serve as inaccurate 'evidence' that our feared consequences are indeed real and about to happen. If this is an experience that you are familiar with don't feel surprised if your body moves into a fight-flight mode in a desperate attempt to escape.

Thoughts and reactions to thoughts that increase the likelihood of catastrophic misinterpretations occurring

Often when we are frightened we use our bodily reactions as evidence that there is something wrong. For example, an increase in heart rate as well as shortness of breath could be used as evidence for the catastrophic thought "I'm having a heart attack" (see figure 9). I have made a list of common misinterpretations in table 1a and table 1b overleaf.

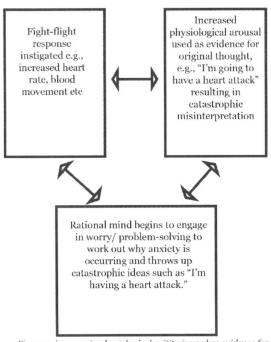

Figure 9. increase in physiological acitity is used as evidence for original cataestrophic thoughts

Research

In 2012 researchers Bethany Teachman, Craig Marker and Elise Clerkin recruited 43 participants with a diagnosis of panic disorder to take part in a 12-week CBT program. They monitored their subjects at frequent intervals looking particularly at changes in catastrophic misinterpretations as treatment progressed. At the end of their study they were able to use their results to predict that the more that panic sufferers changed their catastrophic misinterpretations, the less frightening and more infrequent panic attacks became. In essence their results suggest that cognitive change (i.e., a change in thinking) predicts better treatment outcome.

Body change noticed	Catestrophic misinterpretation
Heart rate increase, heartburn	"I'm having a heart attack."
Feeling light headed	"I'm having a stroke, I'm going to faint." "I'm going to fall over."
Contraction of the digestive system	"I'm going to wet myself, lose control of my bowels."
Blurry vision	"I'm going blind, I'm going to black out."
Increase in sensory activity	"I'm going insane, I'm going to lose control."
Loss of feeling in extremities	"I'm having a stroke."
Rapid breathing	"I'm going to suffocate."

Table 1a. Examples of bodily changes and associated catastrophic misinterpretations

Body change noticed	Associated worry
Heart rate increase, heartburn	"It's happening again. I'm going to have a panic attack."
Shift in breathing tempo	"I've got to control this somehow."
Heightening of sensations	"What's wrong with me"… "Is it always going to be like this"… "If I feel like this now how will I cope with my job"… "I won't be able to function"… "I won't be able to work."

Table 1b. Examples of bodily changes and associated worry about having a panic attack

Chapter summary

Worry, and panic

- A body change occurs e.g., heart is beating rapidly.

- A search for meaning about the experience follows e.g., "Why is this happening to me?" "Is this a sign of a serious problem?" "How do I deal with it?"

- Catastrophic thinking develops as a consequence of searching for meaning e.g., "I could be having a heart attack!"

- Catastrophic thoughts are accompanied by an increased physiological response leading to the individual thinking that the thoughts are real, i.e., catastrophic misinterpretations occur.

Chapter 6 - Homework

You may find it useful to keep a record of your panic attack experiences in the early stages. I have placed some record sheets on the next few pages (see table 2). After your panic attack experience observe what you were doing, the thoughts you had, and how intense your panic experience felt out of 10 (with 10 being the most intense your panic attack could possibly be). After you have made a record of your experience have a look at your thoughts section and assess if you had any catastrophic interpretations. If you did, which ones did you have?

Table 2. Thoughts and catastrophic misrepresentations

You may find it useful to keep a record of your panic attack experiences in the early stages. Notice what you were doing, the thoughts you had and how intense your panic experience felt out of 10 (with 10 being the most intense your panic attack could possibly be). After you have made a record of your experience have a look at your thoughts section and assess if you had any catastrophic interpretations. If you did which ones which ones did you have?

Date/Time	Trigger	Thoughts, e.g., "I can't breath" "I'm going to suffocate"	Panic rating 0 to 10	Catastrophic misinterpretation
8 am 27th June	Woke up with heart racing	I shouldn't be feeling like this, I've only just woken up. There's something wrong with my heart	8	I could have heart disease I might be having a heart attack

Table 2. Thoughts and catastrophic misrepresentations

You may find it useful to keep a record of your panic attack experiences in the early stages. Notice what you were doing, the thoughts you had and how intense your panic experience felt out of 10 (with 10 being the most intense your panic attack could possibly be). After you have made a record of your experience have a look at your thoughts section and assess if you had any catastrophic interpretations. If you did which ones which ones did you have?

Date/Time	Trigger	Thoughts, e.g., "I can't breath" "I'm going to suffocate"	Panic rating 0 to 10	Catastrophic misinterpretation

Table 2. Thoughts and catastrophic misrepresentations

You may find it useful to keep a record of your panic attack experiences in the early stages. Notice what you were doing, the thoughts you had and how intense your panic experience felt out of 10 (with 10 being the most intense your panic attack could possibly be). After you have made a record of your experience have a look at your thoughts section and assess if you had any catastrophic interpretations. If you did which ones did you have?

Date/Time	Trigger	Thoughts, e.g., "I can't breath" "I'm going to suffocate"	Panic rating 0 to 10	Catastrophic misinterpretation

Table 2. Thoughts and catastrophic misrepresentations

You may find it useful to keep a record of your panic attack experiences in the early stages. Notice what you were doing, the thoughts you had and how intense your panic experience felt out of 10 (with 10 being the most intense your panic attack could possibly be). After you have made a record of your experience have a look at your thoughts section and assess if you had any catastrophic interpretations. If you did which ones which ones did you have?

Date/Time	Trigger	Thoughts, e.g., "I can't breath" "I'm going to suffocate"	Panic rating 0 to 10	Catastrophic misinterpretation

Increased threat monitoring and panic

One morning David A, a surveyor, entered my office, looking flustered. I had noticed him earlier standing in the waiting area wringing his hands together. Before I had even introduced myself he informed me "I'm so embarrassed to be here!", "I feel really silly!", "I may need to go ... I hope you don't mind if I need to get up and walk out!"

David found it difficult to describe his symptoms, explaining that they had come on suddenly while at work several months earlier. He appeared perplexed by his situation, after being informed by his General Practitioner (family doctor) that he had been suffering from anxiety. Early on in our meeting he clutched his chest and began to breathe deeply, telling me "It's OK just give me a few minutes" as I asked him about the development of his symptoms.

As our meeting progressed it transpired that one of David's main concerns was having a panic attack in front of others, and what others might think of him. He had been monitoring his body for potential signs, and it appeared that very minor changes in his body could escalate into panic symptoms very quickly.

My hypothesis was that David's threat perception centre had been screening for changes in his body associated with anxiety and then firing off his fight-flight process in response to his anxiety symptoms. (As I mentioned in chapter 4, the sub-cortical region of the brain has its own memory store and having encoded David's previous panic attack as a trauma it had started to screen his body for any potential signs of anxiety). David told me that he often monitored his body to see if his anxiety levels were increasing or decreasing. Following this, he used his anxiety level to determine whether he felt able to complete certain tasks such as being able to go to particular social events or to attend certain work events.

David explained that as his anxiety symptoms progressed he took his threat monitoring to a higher level where he would try to monitor himself pre-emptively so that his anxiety didn't take him by surprise. He regularly began to monitor his heart rate by taking his pulse. He constantly assessed how his head felt, in particular how fuzzy his mind was.

In summary, David had started to develop a phobic response to his own symptoms of anxiety. He had become highly vigilant to body changes viewing them as a potential threat. As time passed he had begun to make further associations about how he behaved and what might trigger body changes, such as rising from his seat too fast, walking rapidly, moving from a hot to a cold environment quickly etc. It was almost as if David felt that his panic was lurking in the background waiting to *attack* him at any moment and because of this he needed to be "On the lookout for it." David was extremely keen to know how to 'get rid' of his anxiety or to learn how to 'control it.' As we are beginning to understand and will explore further, attempts to get rid of anxiety or to control it, in fact only exacerbate it further.

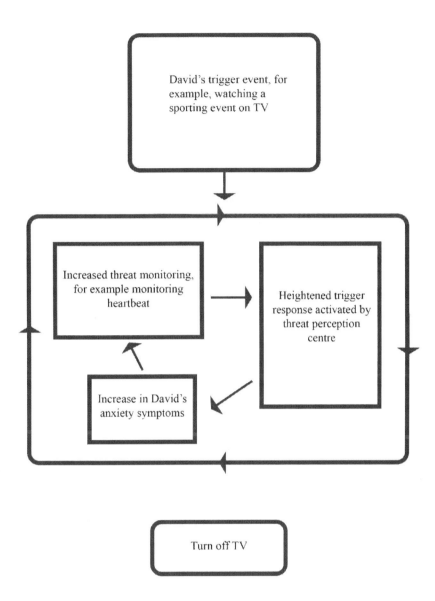

Figure 10. Impact of threat monitoring on David's symptoms of panic.

Chapter summary

Increased threat monitoring and panic

- The threat perception system naturally screens for symptoms of anxiety, especially if a panic attack has been perceived as life-threatening in the past.

- Focusing on changes in the body and viewing body changes as a threat unfortunately increases the intensity of anxiety sensations.

- Regularly screening the body increases sensitivity to feelings and reinforces to the sub-cortical mind that bodily changes are indeed dangerous and a genuine threat.

Behavioural avoidance and safety behaviours

"Oh, just thinking of ways to avoid everyone I work with. And you?"

Paul M. was an Operational Director at a large manufacturing firm. On first meeting Paul he appeared calm, jovial, and relaxed. Paul informed me that the problem he had come to see me about was his difficulty travelling on motorways. His predominant concern was that if he got stuck in traffic and could not leave the motorway he might have a panic attack, lose control, possibly jump out of his car, and run into oncoming traffic.

As our meeting continued Paul disclosed more information about the difficulties that he experienced in the years leading up to his presenting problem. He stated that if he had important upcoming meetings that required a long drive, he would complete practice routes to these destinations at weekends. In order to avoid motorways he drove along country roads. This strategy appeared to be taking up vast amounts of his free time. He stated that it was possible for him to be a passenger in a car but only if his wife was driving as he was worried about how others might react to him feeling panicky. He also informed me that he had not travelled on tubes, busses, or trains for a long time and that he had put off several long-haul flights over the past three years as he also had a slight problem with flying. He told me that he didn't want to work on his flying problem as he was thinking about leaving his current job to work for a company that had no overseas divisions. This would mean that he would not need to fly.

Alongside the above problems Paul mentioned that he found making presentations at work difficult but had managed to get by using **beta-blockers**. A beta-blocker is a drug that blocks the action of adrenaline and noradrenalin on beta-adrenergic receptors, i.e., it dampens the fight-flight response. Paul said that he took a beta-blocker a little while before each big event. A significant problem for Paul was his worry that other people would find out about his problems and judge him negatively based on that.

Further investigation revealed that Paul often rehearsed potential feared scenarios in his mind before they occurred, and worked out strategies that he could use to conceal his anxiety. These strategies involved over-preparing presentations, avoiding drinking tea and coffee in front of others just in case they noticed that his hands might be shaking, and planning potential exits from situations. Paul felt confused about his thinking because on the one hand he thought that people wouldn't really be bothered if he was anxious, while on the other hand he also had thoughts such as "They will think less of me, judge me, respect me less, and view me as weak."

After meeting Paul my initial opinion was that he was quite a long way down the panic attack path as he had several avoidant behaviours and safety mechanisms already in place. I thought that he needed to become more aware of his increasing subtle avoidance strategies and safety behaviours before we could address the root cause of his problems which was his fearful reaction to his own feelings. In fact, Paul had become so successful at avoiding triggers for his panic attacks that he had not experienced a panic attack for over two years before our meeting.

In my clinical practice the types of avoidance and safety behaviours demonstrated by Paul are quite common. Over time many of us develop a range of strategies to control or avoid panic. Many of us feel skilled in dealing with our panic attacks, having become experts in developing ways to avoid them or neutralise them. In many ways this behaviour is easily understandable, not only because our natural inclination is to avoid high levels of fear, which occurs during a panic attack, but also to avoid concerns and catastrophic fears about potential negative social outcomes that could occur as a result of panic.

Conditioned responses to panic

A major problem with using avoidance and safety behaviours where panic is concerned is that the more we carry out safety behaviours the more engrained safety behaviours and avoidance strategies become. We are preprogramed to experience a sense of relief when we carry out a behaviour that removes pain or reduces worry (see figure 11a). In psychological terms this process is referred to as negative reinforcement. (By engaging in a certain behaviour we can avoid experiencing feared negative consequences). Over time as processes are repeated and memory pathways laid down we begin to carry out these behaviours automatically without thinking.

Ultimately, the more that we use avoidant strategies and safety behaviours the less panic attacks we experience. In this respect we feel as though we are dealing successfully with the problem. However, as time progresses more situations that trigger anxiety are likely to occur, leading to more withdrawal. This can lead to a loss of confidence in our body and we may increasingly see our own body as a potential threat. This is accompanied by a feeling of restriction and we may begin to think that there really is something seriously wrong with us, which reduces our confidence still further (see figure 11b). We may even

tell ourselves off for feeling that we are not able to function as a normal person in society and may develop low mood as an added burden.

What is negative reinforcement?

Negative reinforcement occurs when something is removed or taken away (often pain or anxiety) as a result of a particular behaviour. For example, for some people making a decision that they do not need to travel on a plane or a tube can take away their anxiety giving them an immediate sense of relief. Generally, the more an individual uses a behaviour (e.g., taking a pain killer) to remove a stimulus (e.g., pain) the more engrained the behaviour becomes.

Figure 11a. How negative reinforcement develops during a process of avoidance.

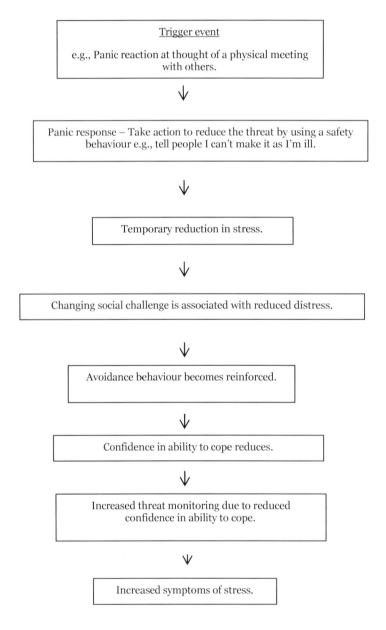

Figure 11b. Impact of avoidance and safety behaviours on symptoms of anxiety.

Chapter summary

Behavioural avoidance and safety behaviours

- Our natural inclination is to move away from or avoid pain (e.g., anxiety).

- Through a process of trial and error we find out what behaviours result in our anxiety reducing (e.g., distraction, avoidance etc.)

- A process of negative reinforcement occurs as our brains make a connection between the use of safety behaviours and feeling relieved.

- Safety behaviours become engrained and automatic over time.

- Our lives become more restricted and our confidence in coping with life events reduces.

- The probability of further panic attacks increases unless further avoidance is utilised.

Chapter 8 – Homework

If you want to, you can use the table on the next page to make a note of the safety behaviours that you use to protect yourself from a panic experience (see table 3). Using table 4, keep a record about how much you believe that this behaviour has stopped something dangerous happening to you or kept you safe. Rate your belief between 0 and 10, where 10 means that you totally believe it.

Table 4. Safety behaviour record

Use this diary to make a note of safety behaviours (e.g., holding onto something supportive) you use each time you have a panic experience. Keep a record also about how much you believe that this behaviour has stopped something happening or kept you safe. Rate your belief between 0 and 10 where 10 means that you totally believe it.				
Date/Time	**Trigger**	**Safety behaviour, e.g., take a Diazepam, sit down**	**Panic rating after safety behaviour**	**How much do you believe your safety behaviour stop something dangerous happening? Score out of 10.**
9th June 12.00 pm	Got up from my seat too fast Felt panicky	Sat down again	6	7

Table 3. Safety behaviours

The following safety behaviours are quite common in panic. Use the box to the left to note which safety behaviours apply to you	✔
Use diazepam (a drug that alters neurotransmitter functioning to produce a calming effect) or beta-blockers before certain situations, e.g., business meetings.	
Carry a supply of diazepam just in case	
Do not move too fast or rest (fear of heart rate increase)	
Drink alcohol before going out to relax	
Avoid situations where a panic attack has occurred in the past or where one may occur in the future	
Do not eat before going out (related to fear of vomiting)	
Go to the toilet before going out (related to fear of losing control of bowels)	
Have someone with you when in potential situations where panic could occur	
Carry a brown paper bag to breath in and out of	
Carry a bottle of water	
Carry a plastic bag (related to fear of vomiting)	
Sit in places near to an exit in public places	
Hold onto or lean onto something supportive	
Hold breath, keep an eye on emotions	
Fan self to stop self over heating	
Distract self, for example watch television	

Table 4. Safety behaviour record

Use this diary to make a note of safety behaviours (e.g., holding onto something supportive) you use each time you have a panic experience. Keep a record also about how much you believe that this behaviour has stopped something happening or kept you safe. Rate your belief between 0 and 10 where 10 means that you totally believe it.

Date/Time	Trigger	Safety behaviour, e.g., take a Diazepam, sit down	Panic rating after safety behaviour	How much do you believe your safety behaviour stop something dangerous happening? Score out of 10.

Table 4. Safety behaviour record

Use this diary to make a note of safety behaviours (e.g., holding onto something supportive) you use each time you have a panic experience. Keep a record also about how much you believe that this behaviour has stopped something happening or kept you safe. Rate your belief between 0 and 10 where 10 means that you totally believe it.

Date/Time	Trigger	Safety behaviour, e.g., take a Diazepam, sit down	Panic rating after safety behaviour	How much do you believe your safety behaviour stop something dangerous happening? Score out of 10.

Table 4. Safety behaviour record

Use this diary to make a note of safety behaviours (e.g., holding onto something supportive) you use each time you have a panic experience. Keep a record also about how much you believe that this behaviour has stopped something happening or kept you safe. Rate your belief between 0 and 10 where 10 means that you totally believe it.

Date/Time	Trigger	Safety behaviour, e.g., take a Diazepam, sit down	Panic rating after safety behaviour	How much do you believe your safety behaviour stop something dangerous happening? Score out of 10.

Connecting the dots

"How could anyone think that this department is under staffed?"

A good deal of information has been covered in this book so far, so it might be useful at this point to have a summary. In chapter 4 the functioning of the threat perception centre was covered. I suggested the function of the threat perception centre is to identify sources of potential threat, whether these are psychological or physical. The threat perception centre will activate the body's alarm system in response to a) direct perceived threats that it notices or b) cues associated with previously perceived or actual threats.

A problem that many individuals with panic symptoms face is that their anxiety experience itself gets encoded within the threat perception centre as a source of threat in its own right. Threat increases further if the rational mind attempts to make sense of anxiety without adequate information. As described in chapter 6, attempting to understand what is going on can often result in the creation of catastrophic misinterpretations e.g., "I'm in danger", "I'm having a heart attack" (see figure 12). Safety-based behavioural responses such as sitting down/resting to prevent a heart attack increase believability of these catastrophic thoughts still further, leading to increased future activation within the threat perception centre. Over time, with repeated use, safety behaviours can become engrained and automatic through a process of negative reinforcement. Breaking or not carrying out **safety behaviours** - precautionary behaviour to prevent feared or bad consequences from occurring - alone can then be sufficient to set off the body's fight flight system (e.g., accidently leaving Diazepam tablets at home).

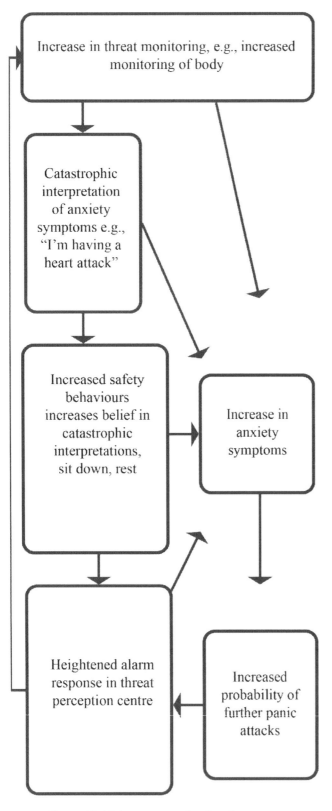

Figure 12. Maintenance cycle of panic symptoms

Chapter summary

Connecting the dots

- Several processes need to work together to maintain symptoms of panic.

- Memories of panic symptoms are stored in the sub-cortical regions' memory bank as a source of potential threat/danger. This can lead to a phobic reaction to one's own feelings of anxiety, which in turn can lead to magnification of anxiety symptoms.

- Using safety behaviours to reduce panic symptoms further reinforces fear triggers.

Challenging catastrophic thoughts

Most people who visit a therapist for treatment for their panic attacks at some point make a visit to a physician with serious concerns about their health. If you have visited a physician and have received an all clear in terms of your health, then it will be useful to begin to understand how symptoms of panic are different to physical problems such as those of a heart attack or a stroke. To do this I'd like us to begin by looking at the evidence.

Am I having a heart attack?

Due to the similarity of some symptoms of panic with those of a heart attack one of the most feared thoughts for people who experience panic is that they are having a heart attack. When experiencing panic our heart rate may rise to a level similar to that experienced while jogging. As panic feelings often tend to occur when we are physically inactive, there is usually no 'obvious' reason for an increased heart rate, and the experience can therefore feel very frightening.

If an increase in your heart rate is viewed as a threat then your amygdala will authorise the release of more threat-based hormones into your body, maintaining a high heart rate, or increasing your heart rate still further. A heightened auditory experience can also lead to a feeling that your heart is beating very loudly. As breathing patterns change, more tension can be carried in the rib cage and this can create spasms within the **inter-costal muscles** - which are very small muscles between the ribs. To a panic sufferer this can feel like chest pain, which leads many people to think they are having a heart attack.

Many of us may engage in safety behaviours when we experience panic attacks, for example, sitting down, having a glass of water, distracting ourselves. You may need to remind yourself that these strategies are not known to prevent a heart attack or heart disease, although they do offer temporary relief from panic.

Am I having a stroke or am I going to faint?

Focussing on the experience of being light-headed, or noticing a lack of sensation in the extremities, such as the finger tips can lead many individuals to think that they are having a stroke. Increased thoughts that you are having a stoke can lead to more intense symptoms of anxiety and a feeling of **dissociation** – this is where you may feel so light-headed that you no longer feel as if you are in your body. Dissociation is a natural protective function that the body produces to help it to come to terms with high degrees of pain or psychological distress. Light-headedness can also occur as a result of **rapid shallow breathing** – which basically involves breathing too fast and breathing out too much carbon dioxide. The loss of feeling in the finger tips and toes is a natural part of the body's fight-flight

mechanism, as blood supply is diverted to major muscle groups.

A real experience of a stroke is very different from panic. If you are having a stroke your face may drop to one side and there may be a droop in your mouth or one of your eyes. You may not be able to lift up one arm because of weakness or numbness. Your speech may be garbled or slurred. You may also experience an extreme headache, suddenly lose your vision, or become unable to talk or understand what others are saying. As with fear of a heart attack, behaviours such as sitting down, having a drink of water etc., are not known to prevent a stroke although they do offer _temporary_ relief from panic symptoms.

A few facts about fainting may also be helpful at this point. Fainting is generally most likely to occur when an individual experiences low blood pressure rather than high blood pressure. Low blood pressure can result in a reduction of oxygenated blood to the brain, which then results in a loss of consciousness. Blood pressure increases during a panic attack which ironically makes fainting less likely rather than more likely. If you have fainted during a panic attack then it may be advisable to consult a physician, as there are a number of medical factors which can cause individuals to faint. Fainting is a common problem for individuals who experience a phobic reaction to blood. This is an evolutionary response which is designed to bring blood pressure down to reduce potential blood loss.

Am I going mad?

"Joe took the day off to go to the ball game. I'm his dog, I'll be sitting in for him until he returns."

A large proportion of people who experience a panic attack think that they are experiencing potential signs of mental illness. Many people have told me that they fear being transferred to a psychiatric hospital. They also think that their symptoms of panic are a sign that they are beginning to lose touch with reality.

Mental health specialists are experts at assessing panic and do not categorise panic as a severe mental illness. Individuals are not sent to psychiatric hospitals for experiencing a panic attack, nor are they sectioned under the Mental Health Act. In fact, panic attacks are considered by mental health specialists as one of the most straightforward, low risk, mental health problems to treat. I am not saying this in any way to minimise your symptoms because your distress may be very severe. I just want to reinforce to you that panic symptoms are not viewed as high risk in terms of their potential to cause you harm.

Am I losing control?

Many clients have told me that they fear panic attacks because they think that they may lose control in some way. Perhaps run down the street naked, assault or hurt others, or humiliate themselves in some way. Although many of us who experience a panic attack do indeed have thoughts about this occurring, (which in turn means that perhaps hundreds of millions of other people also have such thoughts), there is not one account of such behaviour documented in the literature as a result of a panic attack.

Am I am going to throw up?

Many of us may feel nauseous when experiencing panic. This occurs as blood supply is quickly diverted from the digestive system to the major muscle groups. If this is one of your thoughts, I'd like you to ask yourself a question now - How many times have you involuntary vomited while feeling symptoms of panic? Although many people feel nauseous, involuntary vomiting rarely occurs. A far more common reaction for some people who fear vomiting is to go somewhere quiet and make themselves sick. A slight problem with this behaviour is repeatedly engaging in this activity over time can lead to an increased ability to vomit 'almost' involuntarily.

Am I going to lose control of my bowels or wet myself?

As with feeling nauseous, feeling symptoms of panic can make us feel that we need to visit a bathroom. This occurs because movement of the body's resources away from the digestive system leads to a feeling of constriction in those areas. Although many individuals fear that they may lose control of their bowels I have never heard of this occurring unless the person concerned has had a co-existing stomach bug or a weakening of their **sphincter muscles**. Sphincter muscles are muscles that surround the urethra/anus.

I can't breath – I'm going to suffocate!

A common problem that people have when they experience symptoms of panic is to breathe more rapidly. We breathe more rapidly as we need more oxygen to be carried to the muscles to aid their ability to take action to face a threat. A bi-product of this process can be that we end up breathing out too much carbon dioxide. If this occurs the delicate balance between oxygen and carbon dioxide in the body is upset, which leads to rapid breathing or hyperventilation. This experience feels very uncomfortable, but it is in fact harmless. In this state many individuals become concerned they are going to run out of oxygen especially if they are confined within a room or a closed space. Most rooms are not **hermetically sealed.** Hermetically sealed means that the room is designed to block the entry and exit of air. Most rooms even if they are hermetically sealed would have enough oxygen to breathe for hours. It may be useful to bear in mind that if your body is in a state of hyperventilation, then in fact, it has too much oxygen rather than too little. This is why some individuals breathe into a paper bag to build up their carbon dioxide levels when they experience hyperventilation.

Chapter summary

Challenging catastrophic thoughts

- When catastrophic misinterpretations occur they are often accompanied by high degrees of emotional distress.

- Focusing on specific symptoms of the panic response, such as a racing heart, leads to symptoms being used as evidence that there is something seriously wrong.

- Educating yourself about what happens when the body goes into panic is an important first step in managing your symptoms. Reminding yourself about the evidence is the next. For example, can sitting down prevent a heart attack or a stroke?

Some key terms

Luckily there are several different ways to intervene with panic symptoms. They can be challenged by a) understanding much more about how panic works, b) behavioural interventions, c) cognitive interventions and d) using a combined cognitive and behavioural approach. I would like to define these key concepts for you now, so that you become familiar with them.

Behavioural strategies

Behavioural strategies are often used in the early stages of treating panic symptoms. This might mean making a small adjustment to what you do or to alter your environment in some way. Often, the use of behavioural strategies can bring anxiety levels down sufficiently so that other cognitive strategies work more successfully.

Cognitive strategies or interventions

Cognitive interventions are essentially strategies that you can use mainly within your mind. In particular, cognitive interventions require you to react differently to your thoughts and feelings. Cognitive strategies tend to work more successfully when anxiety levels are lower. This is because (as I mentioned earlier) the neocortex (which is used more so for cognitive approaches) tends to go off-line (has reduced capacity/capability) at times of heightened anxiety.

Cognitive behaviour therapy

To make permanent changes to your symptoms of panic you will eventually use a combined cognitive and behavioural approach. This will involve using your new cognitive and behavioural tools while you approach previously feared situations. You will read about this in chapter 14 when I present you with an opportunity to reprogram your sub-cortical mind, or at least help it become less active in situations that currently produce high levels of fear.

Chapter summary

Some key terms

- Behavioural strategies will require you to make changes to your behaviour and to measure the impact of those changes.

- Cognitive strategies are designed to be interventions that you use with your mind.

- Cognitive behavioural strategies are a combination of both the above.

Creating your own hypotheses

A **hypothesis** is a prediction about what you think will occur based on what you think you know. Most of us create hypotheses all of the time in our daily interactions with others. We make hypotheses when we think about how others may think or behave in response to what we do. For example, when I'm in my car queuing in traffic and I want to move into the next lane I know that if I put my indicator on and start edging out slightly, eventually there will be someone who is generous enough in spirit to let me move in front of them.

In my work with clients I also follow a hypothesis driven approach. By this I mean I continuously make educated guesses about what is troubling someone using the information that they have given me. Equally, I actively encourage my clients to engage in a process of making predictions about how they might think, feel, and behave in various situations. In the chapters that follow, you will be offered a chance to test several things out, to create new psychological explanations – or psychological formulations - that will help you move forward in managing your anxiety and panic attacks.

After you understand what is happening to you, you will then be better placed to try out new coping strategies while you are in situations that make you feel anxious. An idea behind carrying out new strategies is to help you find out if making little changes here and there produces different results. I can't stress how important it is that you give yourself the opportunity to try alternative strategies to assess what impact they have on the way you feel. When this occurs you will be able to a) learn from your new experiences and b) repeat similar processes in the future, hopefully even for the rest of your life. Expect resistance from yourself when you complete CBT. Recognise also that if you can pass through this resistance you may learn new things from your experiences. You can also use what you learn in the future, hopefully even for the rest of your life.

To illustrate this I'd like you to imagine there's a fictional reader of this book called John Miller. Let's say that John has been experiencing panic attacks for several months and he has now picked up this book and is reading it. Based on the information offered, John creates a hypothesis that many different areas of his life have had an impact on his experience of panic. After reading chapter 14 he makes a predication that if he reacts to his feelings in a different way his anxiety is likely to reduce. Once John has this prediction in place (i.e., his new hypothesis) he is reluctant to test it out as it is unfamiliar to him. Eventually, however, he allows himself to get curious enough about what may occur if he behaves differently. After John has tested out this new idea he **reflects** – which means that he thinks about the changes that he has noticed. This process of reflection helps John to

firm up his new approach in his mind which in turn encourages him to repeat similar approaches later on.

Fear of change

In my twenty or so years as a psychologist fear of change has cropped up frequently in my professional life. Embarrassingly, I will admit to you now that I initially resist learning new therapeutic approaches thinking my current approach is the best way. I then approach the new therapy area and feel fear, anxiety, and uncertainty while I learn to practice it. At this point these new approaches represent a challenge to my previous view of what I thought I knew and I feel generally incompetent. I then gain the necessary knowledge about using the new approach and my confidence in using it increases. The process then starts over again. Each time I do this I learn new things to extend my knowledge and understanding.

Although CBT is logical and scientific, carrying out CBT approaches will be a challenge to you. Changes in thinking do not happen that readily. Even when change is regarded as good, our natural human tendency is to put up resistance. When you experience this resistance, recognise that your resistance is part of a process of learning. Use it to take you forward. When you take yourself forward your learning will become **experiential** as well as logical. Experiential learning means learning by doing, rather than learning about something by reading or thinking about it.

Chapter summary

Creating your own hypotheses

- We use hypotheses to make predictions about what we think will occur based on the knowledge we have.

- We tend to fear change and put up resistance when we are faced with doing something we don't fully understand.

- A process of significant change moves through a predetermined order – Uncertainty, experiential learning, and then reflection, which in turn leads to a new level of certainty.

Observe yourself

To use CBT effectively you will need to begin observing yourself. The first thing that I will invite you to notice is that you are having thoughts and feelings. The second thing that I would like you to recognise is that you have a range of thoughts, feelings, and behaviours in different circumstances. Once you become aware that your thoughts and feelings fluctuate, you can monitor how you react in different situations. One of the best and most accurate ways to complete self-observation is by writing things down using CBT diaries/worksheets.

Ideally you will approach your thoughts with an intention of becoming really curious about what you will notice. Try to develop an interest in the different types of thoughts that you experience and the feelings or sensations that accompany your thoughts. Carrying out self-observation is not designed to encourage you to judge yourself: Bear in mind that noticing a critical or self-judgemental thought is very different to listening to or believing a thought.

When I first had CBT, I had an aversion to writing and filling in charts. Writing things down didn't really appeal to me. I thought that it might work much better for others, but not for me. Eventually, my therapist Jenny convinced me to fill in the sheets and I found that they actually helped with my mood. I noticed I could stand back from myself more. I started to realise I had many more feelings than I previously thought. I saw that a lot of the things I was doing in my personal life I didn't actually enjoy. I started to see that there were things missing from my life. I wasn't consciously aware of these things before I started observing myself. Once I realised there was a primitive – or feeling - part to the mind, I began to notice when it came on-line much more and how it affected the way that I thought. I recognised that my analytical mind and my feeling mind didn't always agree. I started listening to both parts of my mind and then making decisions after thinking about my life in a more balanced way.

It wasn't obvious to me before I began observing myself that for every thought, feeling, or behaviour I noticed, I had a choice about how to react or respond. Before CBT, I was just living a bit like a puppet, acting automatically. It also helped me not to judge my thoughts and feelings. I felt so much more confident once I noticed I didn't need to react to every thought or feeling that I had.

Self-observation as a scientific approach

A fundamental aspect of any scientific approach is accurate observation. From a CBT perspective, if you are able to stand back mentally and think about your own thinking processes, this will enable you to increase your awareness of your thoughts, feelings, and behaviours, particularly when you are feeling anxious. This process of self-observation will assist you to become aware of the cycles that you engage in when you become anxious.

From this point on I am going to use the term **physiological reactions.** When I use these words I mean specific bodily changes that occur in our bodies. Specific body changes

that you may notice when you are anxious could be increased tension, emptiness, a tight chest, a pounding head, your heart racing, heavy feelings in the legs, and such like. When I use the word **emotions**, I mean it as a way of labelling and giving meaning to specific bodily changes. Many physiological reactions connected to emotions are very similar. For example, the physiological changes associated with anxiety and anger both involve a) heart rate increase, b) a rise on blood pressure, c) tension in major muscle groups, and such like. However, similar bodily reactions can be perceived very differently, and trigger different consequential behaviours.

There are many different variations of self-observation diaries used in CBT, but most involve recording combinations of thoughts, physiological reactions, feelings/emotions, and behaviours. Diaries encourage the use of regular body scanning, which will be beneficial to you as body scanning a) evokes greater sensory awareness and b) encourages increased experiential learning. I mentioned earlier that experiential learning occurs when people learn through their senses and feelings, rather than through thinking or reading.

If you would like to look at an example of a thought, feeling, and behaviour sheet that people fill in when they have CBT, I have copied a typical example onto the next page, (see table 5).

Table 5. Example of Situation, thought, feeling, and behaviour sheet

Situation	Thoughts (e.g., telling someone something that might hurt their feelings).	Emotion (e.g., feeling anxious) and reaction in body.	Behaviour (e.g., avoid the other person).
Walking up a hill	"I can't breathe…I'm going to suffocate"	Anxiety	Stop and have a rest

Can self-observation increase the effectiveness of the pre-frontal cortex?

The brain is well-known by **neurologists** - who are medical experts in the brain - to have high levels of **plasticity**. Plasticity means that the brain has the ability to repair itself and grow in size the more that it is used. Neuropsychologist, Professor Eleanor Maguire from Ireland has published over 100 research articles and book chapters on the neuropsychology of the brain. The majority of her research has focussed on memory, the hippocampus (an important brain area connected to memory) and the sub-cortical brain regions surrounding it. In perhaps one of her most famous papers dating back to the 1990's, she and her colleagues reported the results of their investigation into the brains of London taxi drivers. London taxi drivers were a very useful 'real life' experiment at the time, as there was a requirement that all taxi drivers complete a process known as the 'knowledge.' This required London taxi drivers to spend a large amount of time memorising the spatial layout of London streets - or exercising their hippocampi. If they did not pass the 'knowledge' test they could not become a taxi driver in London. Eleanor Maguire used a process known as structural magnetic resonance imagery (MRI) - a type of brain scan - to measure the hippocampal sizes of participating taxi drivers. She found that London taxi drivers had significantly larger hippocampi than matched non-taxi drivers of a similar level of intelligence and driving experience, and the more experience a taxi driver had, the larger their hippocampus was. Eleanor Maguire's results were ground-breaking to the world of psychology as they demonstrated that there was the potential to grow and strengthen any brain area through the use of cognitive exercise.

Advice on using thought diaries

A key area for you to develop when completing diaries is noticing the thoughts that you have in your mind.

If you find that using thought diaries acts as a trigger for you to worry then you are best off discontinuing using thought diaries, initially. You can return to them later on when you have learned how to use other cognitive exercises - covered later in this book. You may also find that you are not able to complete thought records when you feel really distressed. This is completely normal. If you feel that you can't complete a thought record when you are feeling really anxious, take out a thought record later (when you feel less distressed) and remind yourself about what happened.

Thoughts, physiology, emotion and behaviour diary

Automatic thoughts, e.g. "She doesn't like me"	Physiology, e.g. chest tightening	Emotion, e.g. anxiety	Behaviour, e.g. avoid contact with that person

Thoughts, feelings & behaviour diary

Time: Date: Trigger situation:	Thoughts, e.g. "They must think that I'm an idiot!"	Emotion, e.g. anxiety, anger, shame, disgust	Behaviour, e.g. avoid a situation

Thought, feeling/physiology and behaviour diaries

When you compete self-observation diaries (see tables, 6, 7 & 8) they will a) provide useful material that you can work with and b) act as a low level CBT exercise.

Generally, most of us live our lives automatically, without giving much thought to a) thinking about our thinking, b) how we react to our feelings or c) what makes us behave the way that we do. Completing a diary brings more of these automatic processes into your awareness. Once these patterns are brought into your conscious awareness, you immediately have more choice about how to react. This is due to the fact that writing information down encourages a process of stepping back and observing. This type of detachment will automatically encourage the use of self-reflection. As soon as you start to consider what makes you think, feel, or behave the way that you do, you will be 'working out' the pre-frontal cortex, which can often disengage with anxiety.

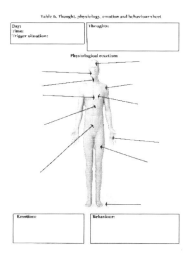

Table 6. Thought, physiology, emotion and behaviour sheet

Table 6. Thought, physiology, emotion and behaviour sheet

Day: **Time:** **Trigger situation:**	**Thoughts:**

Physiological reactions

Emotion:	**Behaviour:**

Table 6. Thought, physiology, emotion and behaviour sheet

Day: Time: Trigger situation:	Thoughts:

Physiological reactions

Emotion:	Behaviour:

Table 6. Thought, physiology, emotion and behaviour sheet

Day:
Time:
Trigger situation:

Thoughts:

Physiological reactions

Emotion:

Behaviour:

Table 7. Thoughts, physiology, emotion and behaviour diary

Automatic thoughts, e.g. "She doesn't like me"	Physiology, e.g. chest tightening	Emotion, e.g. anxiety	Behaviour, e.g. avoid contact with that person

Table 7. Thoughts, physiology, emotion and behaviour diary

Automatic thoughts, e.g. "She doesn't like me"	Physiology, e.g. chest tightening	Emotion, e.g. anxiety	Behaviour, e.g. avoid contact with that person

Table 7. Thoughts, physiology, emotion and behaviour diary

Automatic thoughts, e.g. "She doesn't like me"	Physiology, e.g. chest tightening	Emotion, e.g. anxiety	Behaviour, e.g. avoid contact with that person

Table 8. Thoughts, feelings & behaviour diary

Time: Date: Trigger situation:	Thoughts, e.g. "They must think that I'm an idiot!"	Emotion, e.g. anxiety, anger, shame, disgust	Behaviour, e.g. avoid a situation

Table 8. Thoughts, feelings & behaviour diary

Time: Date: Trigger situation:	Thoughts, e.g. "They must think that I'm an idiot!"	Emotion, e.g. anxiety, anger, shame, disgust	Behaviour, e.g. avoid a situation

Table 8. Thoughts, feelings & behaviour diary

Time: Date: Trigger situation:	Thoughts, e.g. "They must think that I'm an idiot!"	Emotion, e.g. anxiety, anger, shame, disgust	Behaviour, e.g. avoid a situation

Rules

In my clinical work I often help my clients to identify the different types of rules that they hold. We all live by rules and most of the time our rules help us. They work automatically in the background of our minds helping us to make our way through cultural conventions and social occasions. We have literally hundreds of rules that guide our behaviour, for example, rules about queuing up, the way we drive our car, what to do when we attend a dinner party, how to use a knife and fork, what clothing to wear on what occasion, etc. Most of the time we are completely unaware of our rules unless someone breaks them; for example, if somebody pushes in front of us in a queue, talks out loud in a library, and so on.

Many of us also have rules that we use to protect ourselves from our deepest fears; for example, "If I don't notice any unusual sensations then I will be OK", "If I feel strong, and in control at all times, then I will be OK."

When I had my CBT I discovered my rules were mainly about how I wanted others to think of me. They were a bit of a surprise to me when I noticed them. I kind of knew they were there in the background but hadn't really thought about them in that way before. My rules were something along the lines of: "If I produce results and I am contributing at all times then I will be OK." And: "If I meet the highest standards at all times then I will be OK." My rules meant that I spent most of my time working and not spending time with my family. If I wasn't working, I felt as though something wasn't quite right. I found it difficult to stop and rest even for five minutes. If I stopped working I felt guilty or anxious. It felt wrong if I wasn't achieving something.

The development of rules

Rules are usually created early in our lives as children and they often help us during that period of time. However, as we grow older, rules can become out of date and **maladaptive**. By maladaptive I mean that our rules can hold us back rather than work for us. If you would like to investigate what your rules are, begin by noticing what you expect from yourself and others. I have placed some examples of rules that some people expect of themselves and others over the next two pages (see tables 12 & 13). I have placed an asterisk next to rules that are commonly associated with panic attacks. If you are having one-to-one CBT it is usually a good idea to identify what your rules are with your therapist. Use the self (see table 9) and others (see table 10) rule lists to make a note of your rules. Rules about the self could be ideas such as "If others are happy with me at all times then I will be OK." Whereas, rules about others could be "If people respect me and listen to me then I will be OK."

Sometimes rules are difficult to recognise. Close friends and family members will help you to notice what your rules are if you ask them. I have put some of my rules below. If when you read them you think that my rules made me particularly difficult to live with and work with, you would be correct. I tended to get irritated, anxious, and angry if my rules were broken, often making life difficult for others as well as myself.

"If nobody is upset with me and everybody likes me at all times then I will be OK"

"If I work hard and achieve at all times then I will be OK"

"If I am in control at all times then I will be OK"

"If I am strong at all times then I will be OK"

"If people are happy with my performance then I will be OK"

"If I am the best at what I do then I will be OK"

"If people don't let me down then I will be OK"

During the time that I struggled the most I took on very difficult tasks and generally worked until I became exhausted. When I wasn't able to work the way I did before I felt guilty about not working and started beating myself up over it. In therapy, when I thought about what was happening it really brought my attention to what I was doing. I thought I was doing all the extra work to help others and my family but obviously it didn't feel that way to them. Ironically, in my valiant attempts to prove to myself that I was OK, I ended up upsetting most of the people that I came into contact with. You can challenge your rules using CBT exercises (see table 11).

Table 9. Rules **(Use the box to the right to note which rules apply to you)**	✓
If I am in control at all times then I will be OK*	
If people are happy with me at all times then I will be OK	
If I do things perfectly at all times then I will be OK	
If I am the best at what I do at all times then I will be OK	
If I don't experience any any unusual bodily sensations then I will be OK*	
If I am feeling good at all times then I will be OK*	
If I am feeling confident at all times then I will be OK	
If I am not blamed for things then I will be OK	
If I show dominance at all times then I will be OK	
If I perform well at all times then I will be OK	
If I am physically well at all times then I will be OK*	
If I am assertive at all times then I will be OK	
If I know what I am doing at all times then I will be OK	
If I know what is going to happen at all times then I will be OK	
If I appear to others as though I know what I am doing then I will be OK	
If I feel safe at all times then I will be OK*	
If I appear competent at all times then I will be OK	
If I show no signs of vulnerability then I will be OK*	
If I am in control of my feelings at all times then I will be OK*	
If I say "Yes" to all requests at all times then I will be OK	
If I am strong at all times then I will be OK*	
If things go wrong it is all my fault	
If I don't let people down then I will be OK	
If I can fix things then I will be OK	
If I am in control of my body at all times then I will be OK*	
Total number of rules endorsed (write number of rules endorsed in right-hand column).	

Table 10. Rules for others **(Use the box to the right to note which rules apply to you)**	✓
If others don't challenge me then I will be OK	
If people are happy with me at all times then I will be OK	
If people around me don't make any mistakes then I will be OK	
If others tell me that I am the best at what I do at all times then I will be OK	
If people around me are happy, calm and relaxed, then I will be OK	
If people around me are polite and respectful then I will be OK	
If people around me are confident then I will be OK	
If others don't criticise me then I will be OK	
If others let me take charge then I will be OK	
If people around me approeciate me then I will be OK	
If people around tell me that I am alright then I will be OK	
If people listen to me at all times then I will be OK	
If people around me know what they are doing at all times then I will be OK	
If others reassure me then I will be OK	
If others show confidence in me at all times then I will be OK	
If others help me feel safe then I will be OK	
If others approve of me at all times then I will be OK	
If others show no signs of vulnerability then I will be OK	
If others put my needs ahead of their own then I will be OK	
If others say "Yes" to my requests when I ask them, then I will be OK	
If I am around strong people then I will be OK	
If others take the blame for mistakes then I wil be OK	
If others don't let me down then I will be OK	
If others can fix things for me then I will be OK	
If others are there for me when I need them then I will be OK	
Total number of rules endorsed (write number of rules endorsed in right-hand column).	

Table 11. Rule challenging exercise

Rule	How old is the rule?	If you gave yourself an opportunity to have another rule, what rule would you pick?

How real and familiar does this rule feel?

Where do you think this rule came from?

What impact does the rule have on your life?

How do you think you might feel if you choose to live by your new rule as much as you did the old one?

If you learnt the rule from a person where do you think he or she learnt it from?

What benefits does this rule have on your life?

How does knowing that you can choose to have another rule make you feel?

Do you want to keep this rule?

Were you born with that rule?

Table 11. Rule challenging exercise

Rule

How real and familiar does this rule feel?

What impact does the rule have on your life?

What benefits does this rule have on your life?

Were you born with that rule?

How old is the rule?

Where do you think this rule came from?

If you learnt the rule from a person where do you think he or she learnt it from?

Do you want to keep this rule?

If you gave yourself an opportunity to have another rule, what rule would you pick?

How do you think you might feel if you choose to live by your new rule as much as you did the old one?

How does knowing that you can choose to have another rule make you feel?

Table 11. Rule challenging exercise

Rule	How old is the rule?	If you gave yourself an opportunity to have another rule, what rule would you pick?
How real and familiar does this rule feel?	Where do you think this rule came from?	
What impact does the rule have on your life?	If you learnt the rule from a person where do you think he or she learnt it from?	How do you think you might feel if you choose to live by your new rule as much as you did the old one?
What benefits does this rule have on your life?	Do you want to keep this rule?	How does knowing that you can choose to have another rule make you feel?
Were you born with that rule?		

Chapter summary

Rules

- We initially develop rules to keep ourselves safe.

- Rules can be difficult to recognise and many of us are unaware that we have them.

- When our rules are broken we usually experience an emotional reaction.

Beliefs

Generally speaking, limiting beliefs are deeply held ideas about ourselves that we fear are true. By the time that we become adults, our beliefs can become so set within us that we feel that they are part of who we are. We may also carry out numerous 'safety behaviours' to protect ourselves from them without being aware of it. Most of us have absolutely no idea that our beliefs are running us.

I discovered that one of my limiting beliefs was: "I am a failure!" The funny thing about it was no matter how hard I worked or how much I achieved, the belief "I am a failure" was always still there. It seemed like what I had done in the past counted for nothing. Trying to prove the belief wrong demanded so much of my time that it affected my health and the happiness of my family. I didn't realise it was driving me so much. I didn't feel in control of my life. It drove me to do more and more. I didn't really know how to stop! My CBT therapist helped me to notice that in many situations I was experiencing high levels of painful emotions that were inconsistent with the situation that I was faced with. For example, we identified that I had an over-the-top reaction to even small amounts of criticism. Using this awareness my therapist helped me to recognise that the belief "I am a failure" which was experienced at a 'felt sense level' was the main driver for my emotional reaction. My extreme distress response was the primitive part of my brain trying to protect me from being a failure.

After this, I became much more observant and aware of my emotional reactions (without judging them) and I usually took a minute out to see if a limiting belief was influencing me. When I became distressed my thinking may have gone something along the lines of: "That's interesting! I'm experiencing really intense feelings right now, but I haven't actually done anything wrong and nothing is going to happen to me. What am I possibly stuck with right now or believing about myself that is making me feel this way?"

"James! Do you think you might be trying to do too much again?"

How do we develop limiting beliefs?

The most obvious ways that we develop limiting beliefs do not really need any scientific evidence or scientific explanation. If parents or caregivers tell their children that they are weak, stupid, worthless, or a failure it is purely logical that most children will develop limiting beliefs! Most of us would understand that children treated in this way would develop a negative view of themselves. In a similar manner,

children can develop limiting beliefs through negative messages from care givers that are implied through action and inaction. Once a child develops limiting beliefs they are usually very difficult to shift and tend to be retained into adulthood.

There are also other ways in which people develop beliefs: ways we might not normally think about. I am saying this because I have come across a large number of clients who appear to have limiting beliefs, yet they cannot recall any significant trauma, and they have no history of parental abuse or poor treatment in their childhood.

The subtle ways that we develop beliefs

In 2014, researchers from the University of Michigan, Jacek Debiec and Regina Sullivan completed some interesting research on rats. They taught young female rats to fear the smell of peppermint by pumping the smell of peppermint into their cages and giving them electric shocks at the same time. The female rats were then left to their own devices for a while, mated, became pregnant, and gave birth. After the mothers had given birth researchers re-exposed the mother rats to the peppermint smell again, without electric shocks this time, while they were with their young. The researchers found that infant rats learned to fear the peppermint smell by noticing the scent of fear given off by their mothers. Brain scans carried out on the baby rats revealed that a fear of peppermint was programmed directly into the infant rats' amygdala. As I wrote about earlier, the amygdala is the seat of our natural response to threat. There is growing evidence that infant children's brains operate in a similar way to baby rats' brains, both in the womb and after birth up until the age of 6 months. Research in this area is still being carried out.

Research findings such as those described above are beginning to suggest at a most basic level that children absorb their parents' fears. The implication is that we are biologically pre-programed to accept a rapid transfer or download of information from our parents. One of the reasons why Jacek Debiec set up his experiments in the first place was because he had come across many people who came to him with nightmares and post-traumatic symptoms connected to the Holocaust. The issue that confused him most of all was that these particular adults with post-trauma symptoms had not even been born during the Holocaust; they were children of Holocaust survivors and somehow and someway they had absorbed the fears of their parents.

Social learning and belief systems

The above methods of learning belief systems are not the only ways that we can develop belief systems. There is also a process called social learning that we will need to give some attention to.

In 1977, Albert Bandura wrote about a process he identified in children called observational learning, which is now more commonly known as social learning theory: He witnessed that children act as little information processers watching and copying the behaviour of important others, or role models. For example, in the foreword to this book I mentioned that my father felt that he needed to do things perfectly and to very high standards. It is a big possibility that I may have learnt this way of behaving from him. A further strong personal clue to this is the number of times my younger brother has said to me "Jim! The problem is ...You're just like DAD!"

Identifying limiting beliefs in CBT

To identify limiting beliefs I usually begin by asking my clients to remember a situation where they experienced quite intense emotions. Clients determine if their emotion is more intense than they think is appropriate for their situation. I then help my clients to complete a CBT exercise called a **downward arrow**. With a downward arrow exercise, therapists help their clients to keep following feelings and thoughts until their clients reach the deepest fears that they hold about themselves. I have put an example of a downward arrow exercise on the next page (see figure 8).

I strongly advise you not to do this exercise by yourself unless you have already completed CBT with a trained therapist.

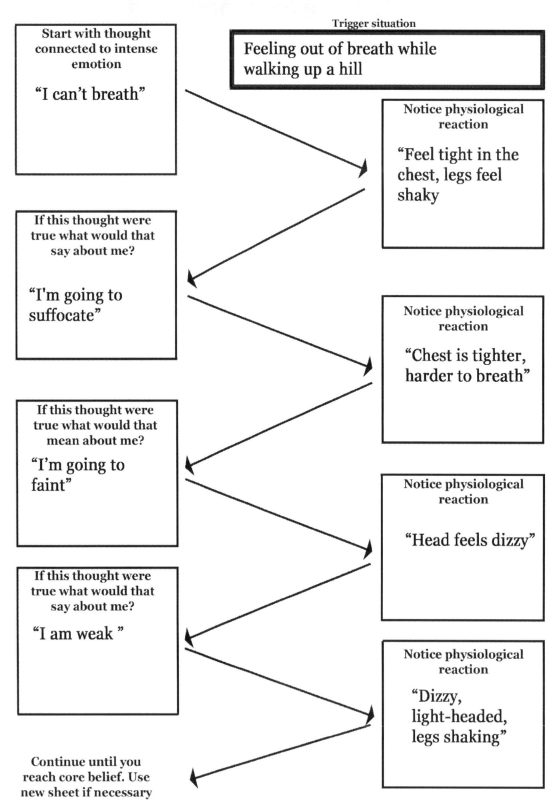

Figure 13. Completed example of a downward arrow

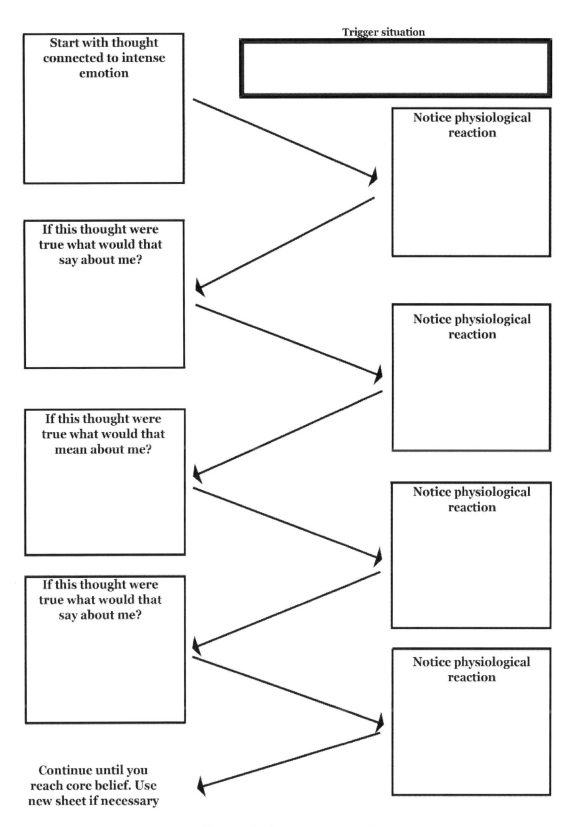

Figure 13. The downward arrow exercise

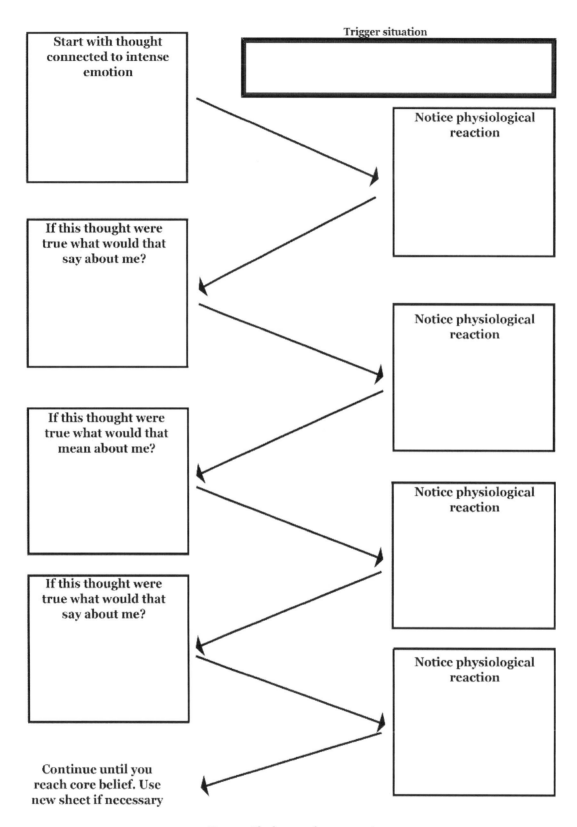

Figure 13. The downward arrow exercise

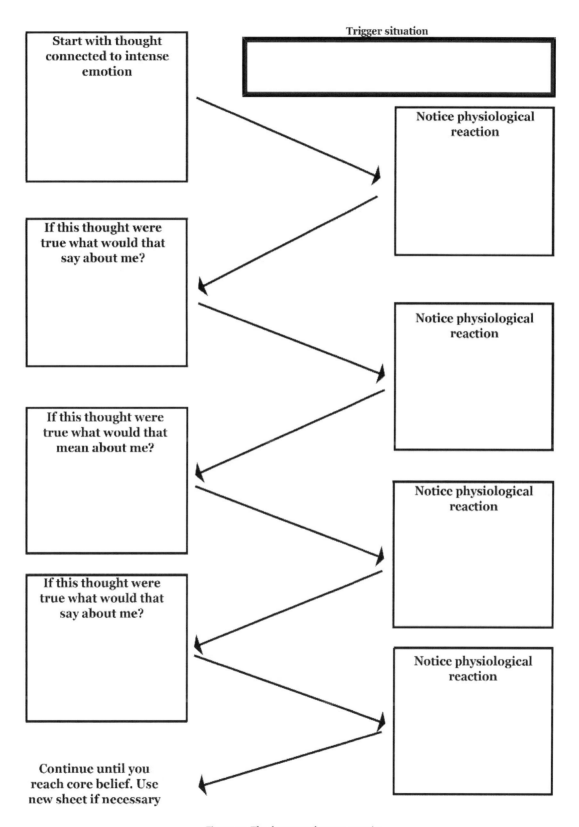

Figure 13. The downward arrow exercise

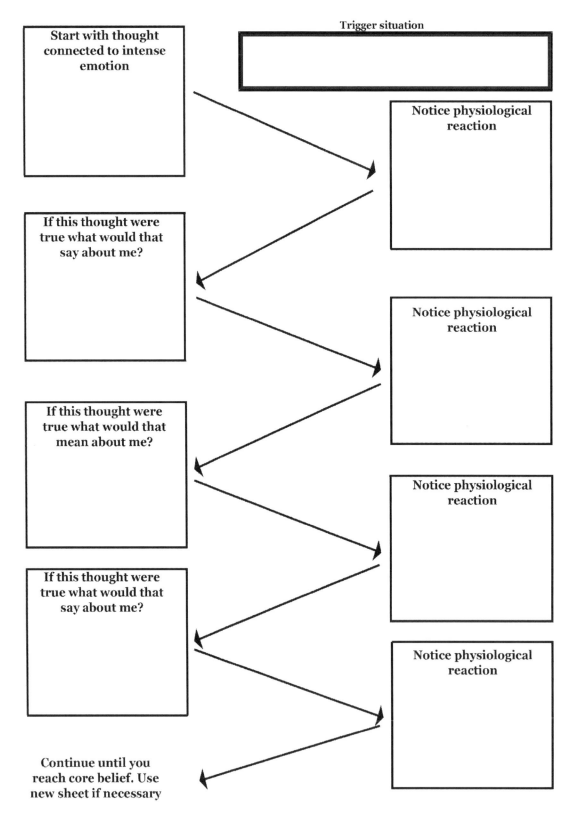

Figure 13. The downward arrow exercise

Chapter summary

Beliefs

- Beliefs are deeply held ideas about the self that we fear are true.

- Beliefs tend to be developed in childhood and we carry them into adult life.

- A downward arrow exercise is often used to identify beliefs in CBT

Drawing out CBT cycles

In my sessions with clients I often draw out cycles using my whiteboard to explain how people's distressing feelings and behaviours are being maintained. A general idea behind drawing out cycles is to help people recognise that some of the things that they do tend to keep their problems in place. Once you realise that you have a cycle in place, you will then need to work out how to break the cycle.

There are several ways to draw out cycles. I'd like us to start with making a connection between beliefs, rules, and safety behaviours. It generally looks a bit like figure 14 on the next page.

Cycle of beliefs, rules, and behaviours

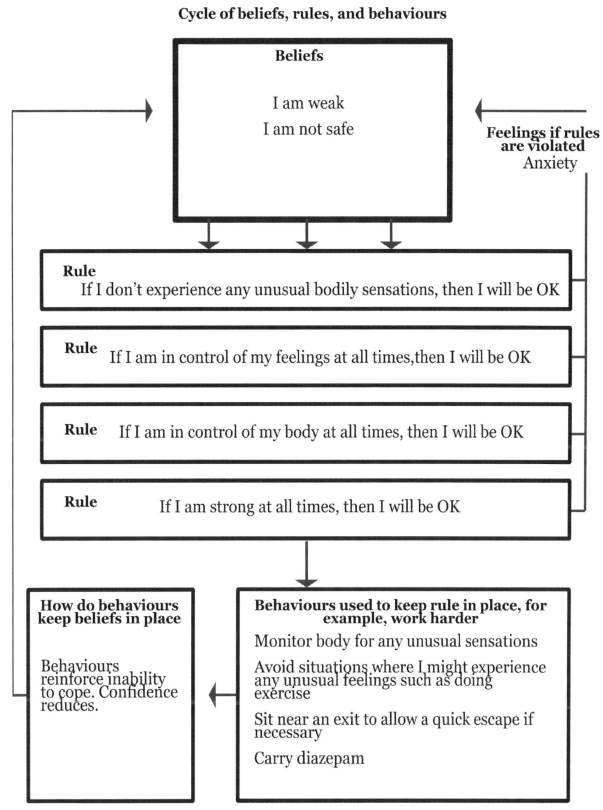

Figure 14. Example of a CBT cycle for panic

Another CBT cycle

The most common CBT cycle is a thought, feeling, behaviour, and physiology cycle. In this cycle, thoughts influence feelings, feelings influence behaviour, and behaviour reinforces thoughts. The whole process works like a vicious cycle.

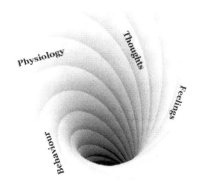

Before you fill in a CBT cycle it is usually practical to write down some of the most frightening thoughts that automatically occur when you panic. For simplicity, from this point on I will refer to your frightening automatic thoughts as FATs. Select one of your most frightening thoughts, verbally repeat the FAT in your mind for a little while and then follow it with a **body scan.** A body scan will involve you bringing your awareness to your body, and noticing physiological changes and emotions that accompany your FAT. The meaning behind your FAT can be identified by asking yourself "If this thought were true, what would it say or mean about me?"

CBT cycles can be especially useful in bringing to mind how **self-fulfilling prophecies** work (see figure 15). This will then naturally lead on to the completion of a FAT challenging exercise, which will be covered in chapter 17. A self-fulfilling prophesy occurs when we spend a significant amount of time and effort trying to prevent something happening, but the very things that we do to stop that something happening actually cause that something to happen.

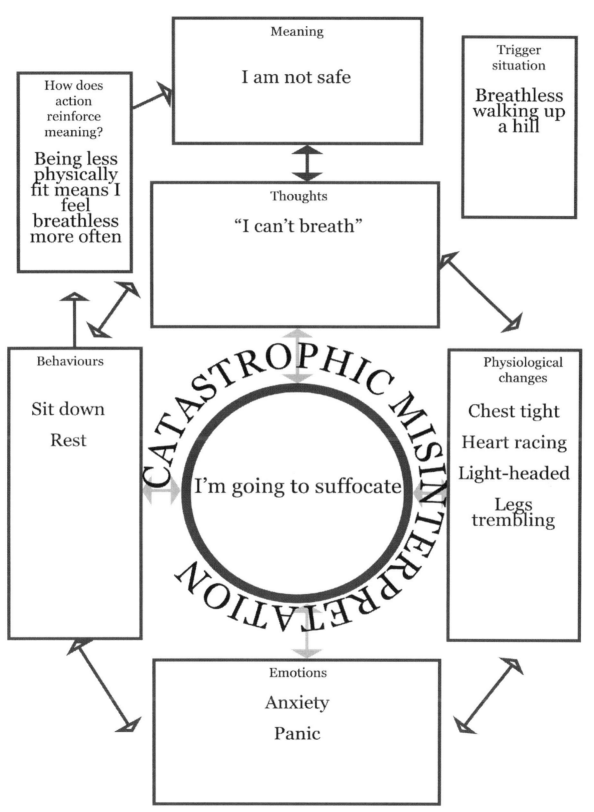

Figure 15. An example of a CBT cycle for panic

Cycle of beliefs, rules, and behaviours

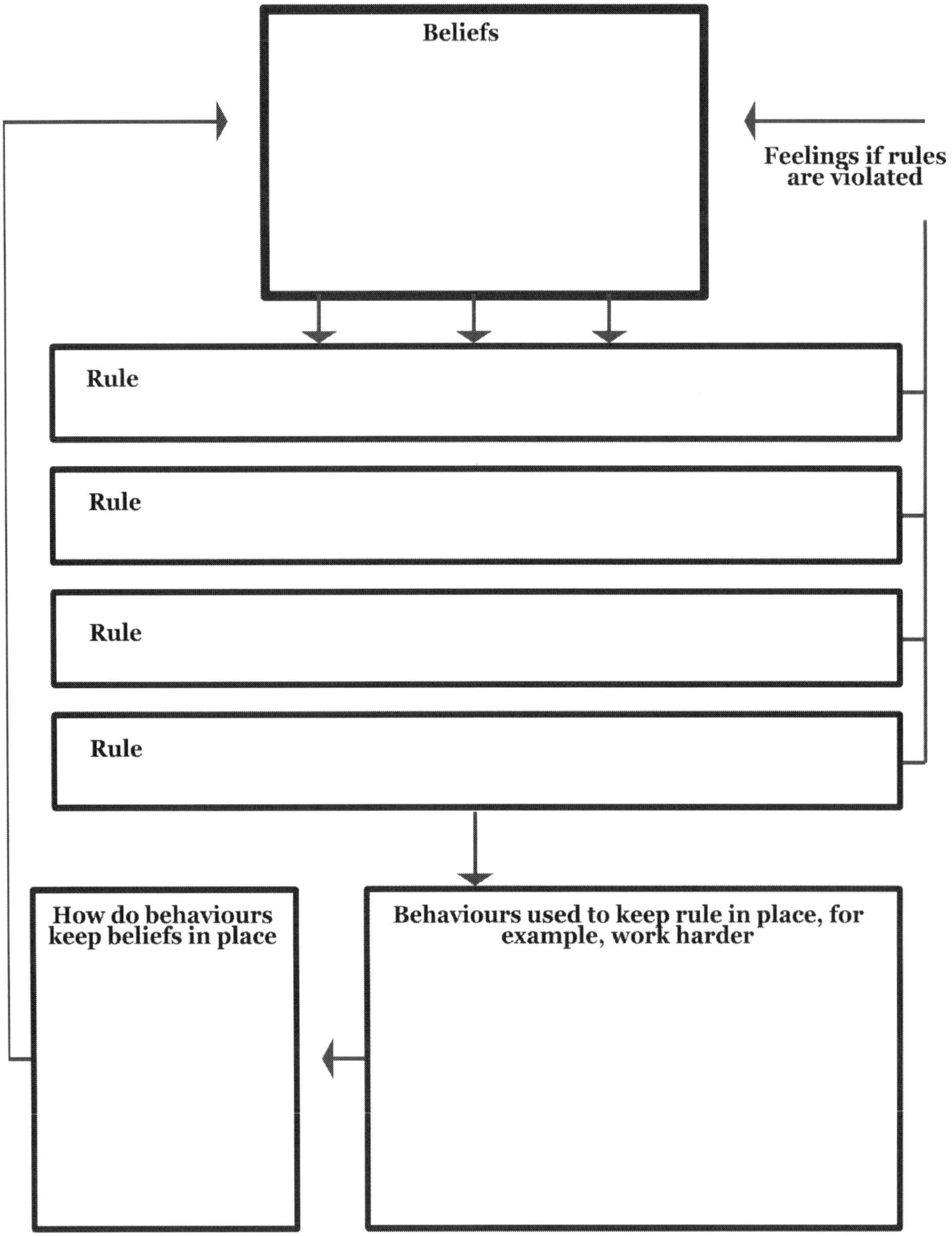

Beliefs

Feelings if rules are violated

Rule

Rule

Rule

Rule

How do behaviours keep beliefs in place

Behaviours used to keep rule in place, for example, work harder

Figure 14. Example of a CBT cycle for panic

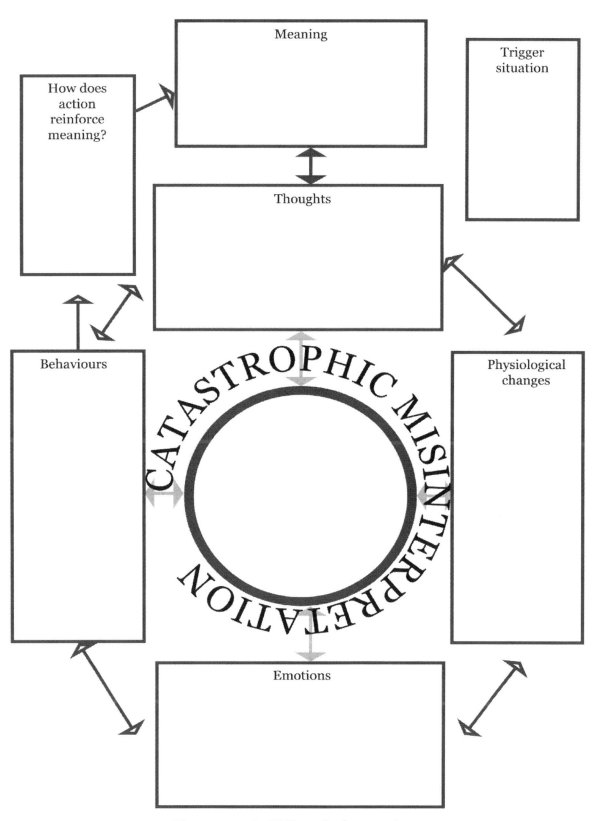

Figure 15. A CBT cycle for panic

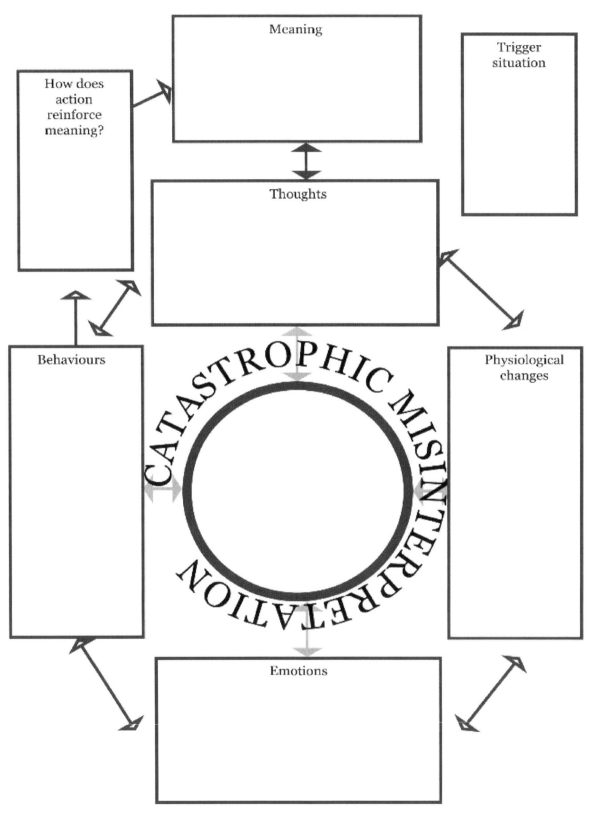

Figure 15. A CBT cycle for panic

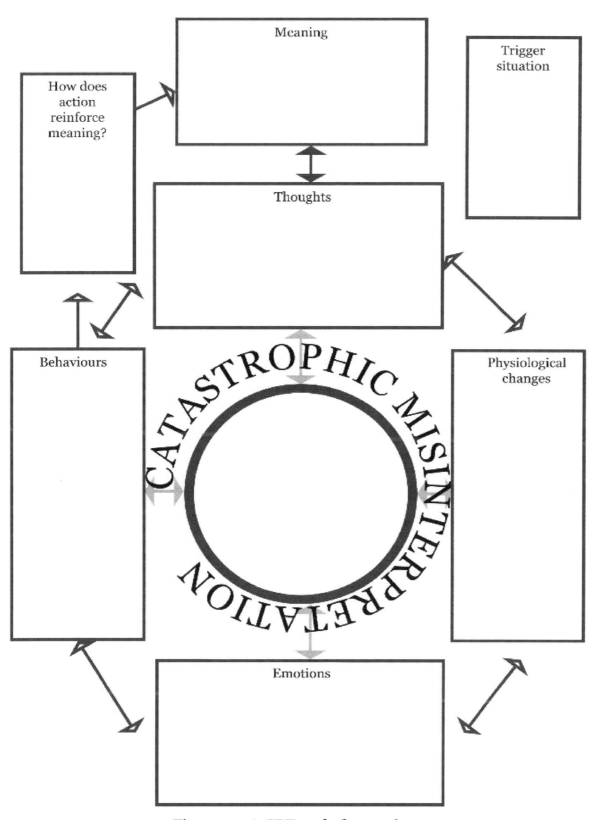

Figure 15. A CBT cycle for panic

Chapter summary

Drawing out CBT cycles

- The most common CBT cycle is a thoughts, physiological changes, emotions, and behaviours cycle.

- CBT cycles can be very useful for demonstrating how self-fulfilling prophecies work.

Challenging FATs

A practice that many cognitive behaviour therapists teach is challenging FATs. As I mentioned earlier FATs are the types of thoughts that run in our minds when we feel panicky or anxious. FATs are important to identify in CBT because they affect the way that we feel. Because of this, it will be very important for you to notice and challenge them as early as possible.

The first stage in recognising FATs is to set aside some time before or after events that provoke more intense anxiety and write down the types of frightening automatic thoughts that come to mind. I have placed a list of common thoughts that panic sufferers have below.

Common frightening automatic thoughts in panic

"I don't think I'll get through it this time"

"I can't breathe"

"What's wrong with me?"

"I shouldn't be feeling like this."

"I'm going insane"

"I'm going to have a stroke"

"I'm going to die"

"Why can't I control this?"

"I'm going to fall"

"I'm going to faint"

"Why am I feeling dizzy?"

What do you do after you notice FATS?

Stage 1. Once you recognise that you have FATs you then have a choice about how you decide to react to them. You can challenge them, or become aware of them and choose not to react to them. Many of my clients find that noticing their frightening thoughts and choosing not to react to them is very difficult, initially. With this in mind, I often find it useful in the early stages to spend time with my clients teaching them how to challenge their FATs. Rebecca one of my clients had a FAT "I'm going to pass out if this doesn't stop very soon." I have placed her information into a cycle, (see figure 16).

Stage 2. The second stage in challenging FATs is to bring alternative explanations to mind using a thought challenging record (see table 13). A thought challenging record is really a collection of notes that you can make to provide alternative evidence against your FATs. FATs are placed in the first column, evidence for the automatic thoughts are placed in the second column, evidence against the FAT is placed in the third column, and an alternative more balanced thought is placed in the fourth column.

Collecting evidence against FATs can sometimes be difficult and because of this it will be important to persist. Some people find it helpful to complete FAT challenging exercises with their therapist. Alternatively, you might ask trusted loved ones to help you challenge your FATs. You could also think about what you might say to others with similar problems to yourself if you were challenging their FATs.

Stage 3. After completing a thought challenging record it is often useful to put the alternative more balanced thought into a positive CBT cycle to look at how it might change things. Please see figure 17 for Rebecca's positive CBT cycle.

NB. FATs have a habit of coming back, so it may be useful for you to get your FAT challenging notes out and re-read them when this occurs.

Look out for cognitive distortions when you challenge your FATs

When we become distressed, the way that we think can change. High levels of distress can distort our perception, mood, and behaviour, directly affecting the way we make sense of things. When this occurs our thinking style can move from being balanced, flexible, expansive, and considering to a more rigid style (see table 12).

Early on in my CBT sessions, I recognised the amount of cognitive distortions I had in my thinking. The best way I can think of to explain it is to imagine that someone puts some glasses on you, but you don't realise that you're wearing them. The glasses can make things seem much bigger or smaller than they really are.

"I'm so glad that you could all make it today..."

When I began work with my therapist she helped me to realise that when I got upset I didn't always see the world clearly. Sometimes I filtered information so that I only saw what my mind would let me see. This meant I had a limited viewpoint and could not see what was really happening in my life!

At other times, I felt really sure that I knew what was going to happen before things actually happened.

"Looks like it's going to be terrible tonight! I think I had better stay in."

And, everywhere I looked I could see danger.

It is vital in your CBT journey that you learn to recognise when cognitive distortions are occurring so that as time progresses you can learn how to detach from them. I have placed a table of some of the more common thinking distortions on the next page for you to have a look at.

I also usually have a speech ready to tell my clients. It goes something like this: The moment we say to ourselves "Nothing ever works for me," "He or she always does that to me" or "I'm never considered," this will become our reality at that moment in time. If it were true that nothing ever worked out, that all people always behave like this to us, all of the time, and that we were never considered, that indeed would be a pretty despairing place to be. Instead, how about if we choose to have awareness, without judgement of our thinking style? This will allow us to quickly acknowledge obvious distortions. This acknowledgement alone can have a marked positive impact on how we feel. Isn't it so much more refreshing to be able to stand back from seeing the "alls" and "everythings" as facts and notice them instead as thinking styles, or momentary beliefs.

Table 12. Cognitive distortions

Thinking biases and what to look out for

All or nothing thinking: Viewing things as either right or wrong; there is no middle ground. Things are either perfect or fundamentally flawed. There is just black or white, grey does not exist, e.g., always/never, good/bad.

Personalising: Focussing on things in the immediate environment and connecting it to the self. Thinking for example, "she did that deliberately because she knew that I wouldn't like that!" The world revolves around the self.

Mental filtering: Selecting specific negative ideas to dwell on and ignoring all of the positive ones.

Disqualifying the positive: Positives don't count, there is nothing special about the way I did it, e.g., "That only happened because I was lucky."

Distorted images: Using images as evidence. A picture or image in the mind that reflects extreme themes of fear, sadness, disgust, pain, etc.

Fortune telling: Predicting the future in a negative way without any real evidence, e.g., "It's going to be terrible", "It will be a disaster", "I just know it."

Shoulds, oughts & musts: Having ideas that things can only be done one way: - "People should ...", "I must ...", "I really ought to ...", "He shouldn't have ..."

Over-generalising: Taking single events or circumstances and viewing them as happening more often than they really do. Thinking that things happen everywhere.

Emotional reasoning: Using emotions as evidence, e.g., "I feel it, so it must be true."

Mind reading: Drawing conclusions about what others are thinking without any evidence, e.g., "She doesn't like me", They think I am stupid."

Table 13. FAT challenging form

Frightening automatic thought, for example, "I am going to die"	Evidence for negative automatic thought, for example, "I feel that it might happen"	Evidence against negative automatic thought, for example, this has never happened before	New more balanced thought, for example, although I feel panicky nothing has happened in the past and is unlikely to happen this time
"I'm going to pass out if this doesn't stop very soon"	I feel shaky My legs feel like jelly My mind feels like it's swimming I feel faint	I'm still standing I've never passed out before Blood pressure goes up during panic making fainting less likely This is just my pre-frontal cortex going off line	My mind does feel faint and like it's swimming. It feels uncomfortable but nothing dangerous is actually happening.

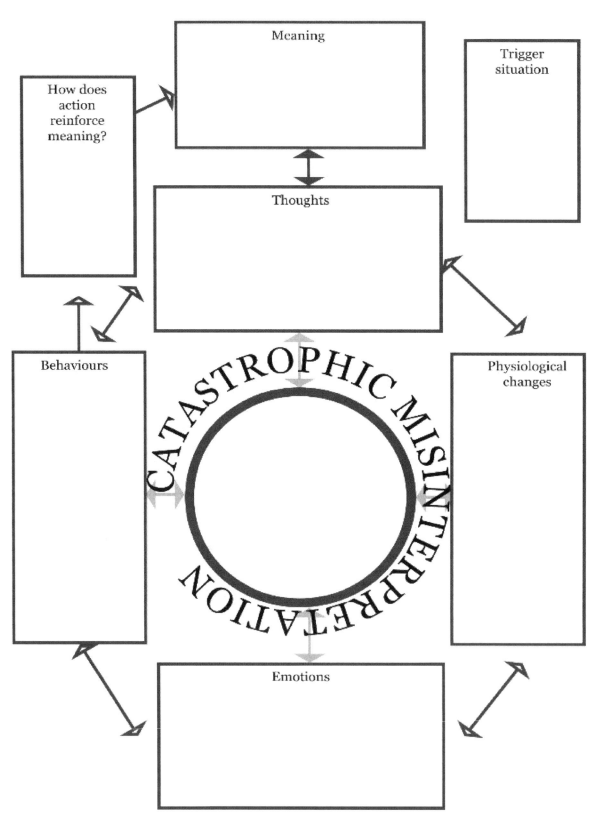

Figure 15. A CBT cycle for panic

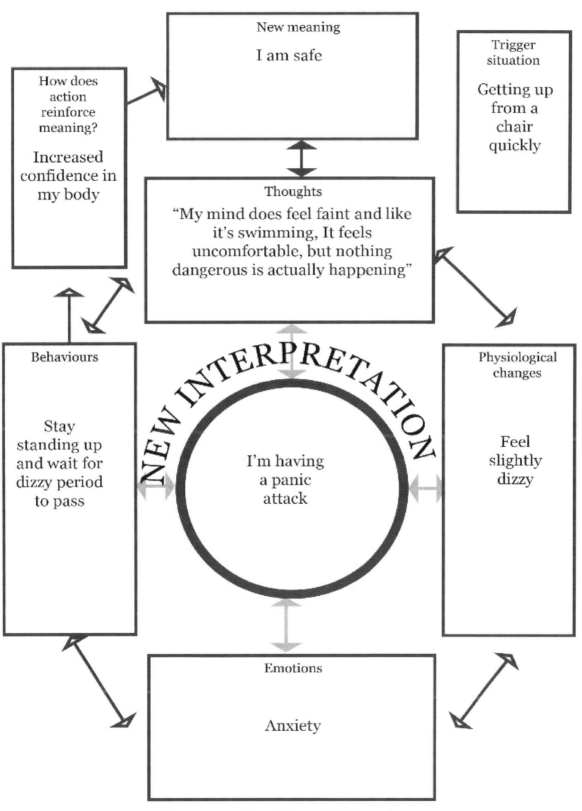

Figure 17. Positive CBT cycle

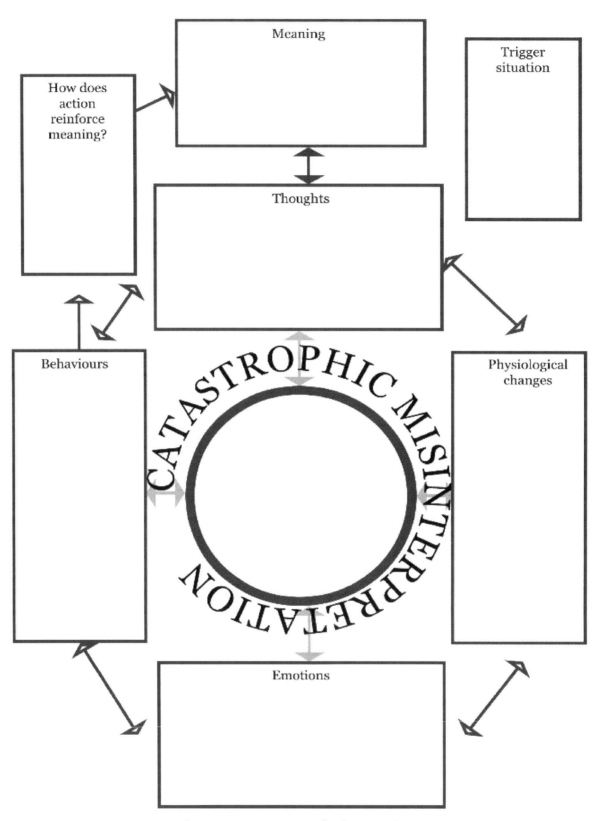

Figure 15. A CBT cycle for panic

Table 13. FAT challenging form

Frightening automatic thought, for example, "I am going to faint!"	Evidence for negative automatic thought, for example, "I feel that it might happen"	Evidence against negative automatic thought, for example, this has never happened before	New more balanced thought, for example, although I feel anxious nothing has happens in the past and is unlikely to happen this time

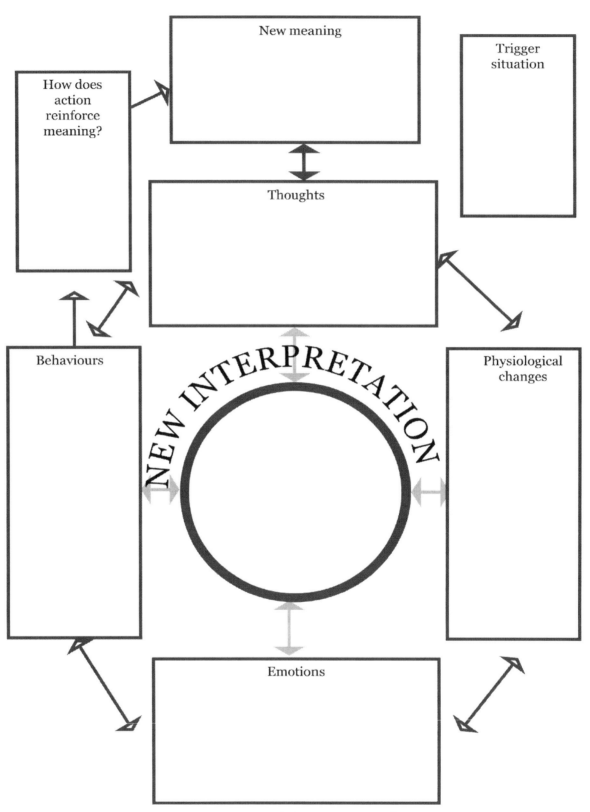

Figure 17. Positive CBT cycle

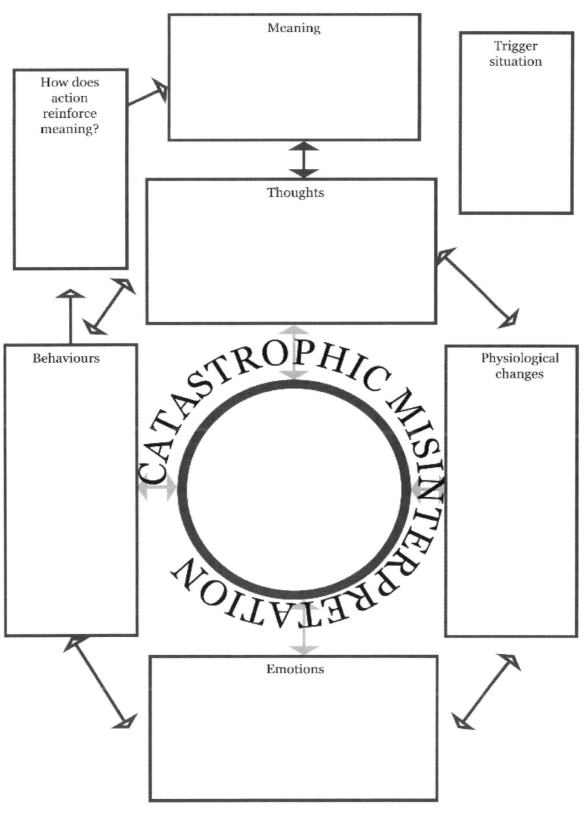

Figure 15. A CBT cycle for panic

Table 13. FAT challenging form

Frightening automatic thought, for example, "I am going to faint!"	Evidence for negative automatic thought, for example, "I feel that it might happen"	Evidence against negative automatic thought, for example, this has never happened before	New more balanced thought, for example, although I feel anxious nothing has happens in the past and is unlikely to happen this time

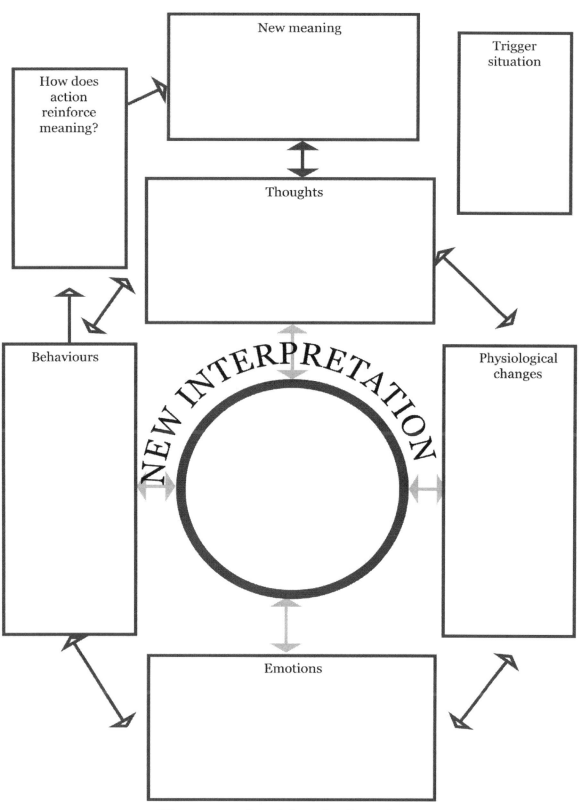

Figure 17. Positive CBT cycle

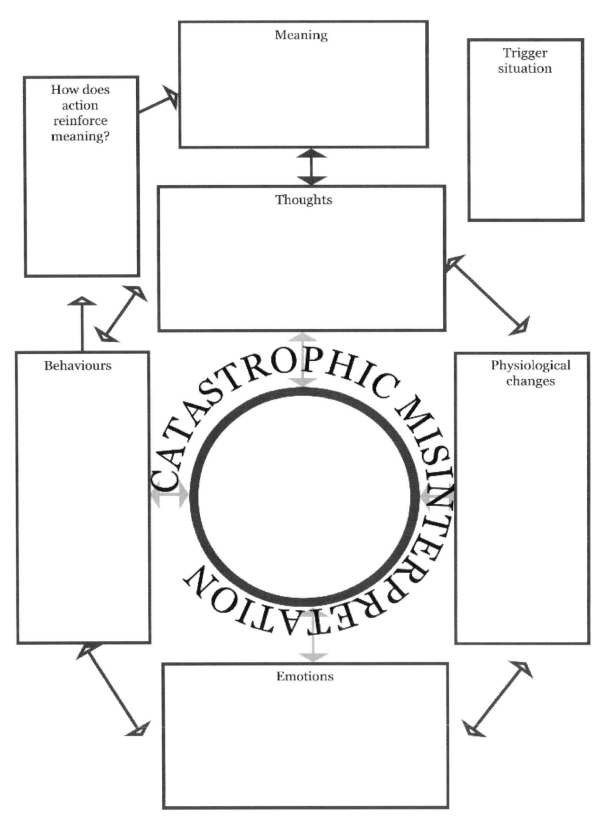

Figure 15. A CBT cycle for panic

Table 13. FAT challenging form

Frightening automatic thought, for example, "I am going to faint!"	Evidence for negative automatic thought, for example, "I feel that it might happen"	Evidence against negative automatic thought, for example, this has never happened before	New more balanced thought, for example, although I feel anxious nothing has happens in the past and is unlikely to happen this time

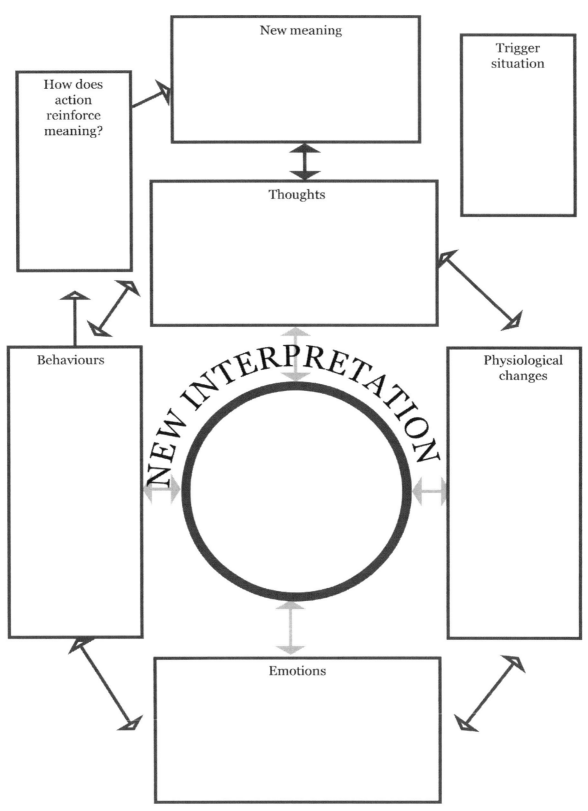

Figure 17. Positive CBT cycle

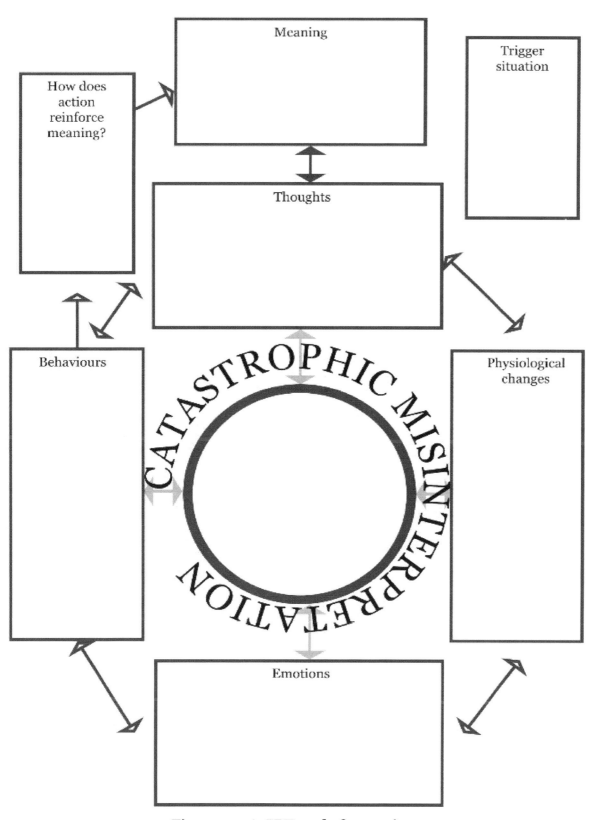

Figure 15. A CBT cycle for panic

Table 13. FAT challenging form

Frightening automatic thought, for example, "I am going to faint!"	Evidence for negative automatic thought, for example, "I feel that it might happen"	Evidence against negative automatic thought, for example, this has never happened before	New more balanced thought, for example, although I feel anxious nothing has happens in the past and is unlikely to happen this time

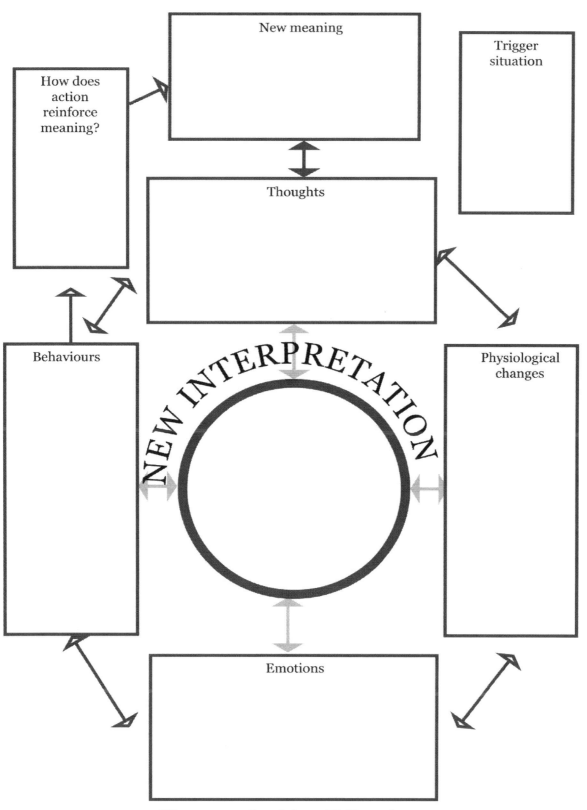

Figure 17. Positive CBT cycle

Chapter summary

Challenging FATs

- The first stage in challenging FATs is setting aside some time to notice the thoughts that are around when you feel very anxious.

- After you have noticed FATs you can just observe them and choose not to react to them, or you can challenge them.

- You can bring alternative explanations against your FATs to mind by using a thought challenging record.

- After you have completed a thought challenging record you can insert your new information into a positive CBT cycle.

- FATs have a habit of coming back so it is often very useful to get your thought challenging records out on a regular basis and spend some time re-reading them.

Short-term behavioural approaches

"The problem is that you're overmedicated.
Luckily there are drugs that can help with that."

If you have just started having panic symptoms there are several things that you can do to help reduce your distress. I recommend that you use the following behavioural strategies on a <u>short-term basis only</u> until you are able to carry out the exercises that I will share with you later.

Temporarily reduce your stress levels

In chapter two I suggested that some individuals with stressful lives can experience high baseline anxiety/stress levels due to a number of factors.

Based on this suggestion it could be helpful for you to look at specific areas where you may be able to temporarily reduce your stress levels, thereby reducing your overall threat response activation. Solutions for stress reduction could be a) working less hours, or b) lessening commitments in various areas. This will make it less likely that you will move into the panic attack critical zone. (I have duplicated figure 2, please see below).

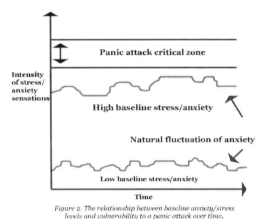

Figure 2. The relationship between baseline anxiety/stress levels and vulnerability to a panic attack over time.

Clinical experience continues to inform me that the more that baseline stress levels can be reduced the easier it is to start treating panic attacks.

Reducing stress levels will not necessarily remove panic but panic symptoms can become less severe.

Other short-term behavioural strategies

There are some other useful strategies that can be used in the early stages of CBT that can also break the panic cycle quite quickly.

Abdominal breathing

One strategy to utilise if you are experiencing panic symptoms is abdominal breathing. Deliberately breathe deeply and slowly, inhaling air to the bottom of your lungs while concentrating on your breath. This will help to prevent hyper-ventilation, one of the main reasons for an experience of dizziness or light-headedness. Breathing more slowly will reduce the amount of carbon dioxide that is leaving your body, and thereby produce a calming effect.

Focussed distraction

A further temporary short-term strategy is focussed distraction. Distraction can be used to prevent negative self-talk and catastrophic thinking. There are a number of different ways of carrying out distraction. One method is to look at the details of everything around you, focussing your attention externally. In this respect you will be looking at the colours, textures, smells, patterns in your surroundings. This is deliberate behaviour designed to intentionally divert your focus away from frightening thoughts and feelings, and towards an awareness of your environment. When you do this ask yourself "What do I see, hear, or notice outside of myself?"

Chapter summary

Short-term behavioural approaches

- Reduce your overall stress levels to bring your baseline anxiety levels down.

- Use abdominal breathing to prevent hyper-ventilation.

- Use focussed distraction to block negative self-talk and catastrophic thinking.

Homework – Chapter 18

It may be useful to keep a note of what happens when you start making behavioural changes to reduce your anxiety (see table 14). Make a note of your anxiety level out of 10 before and after you utilise a short-term behavioural approach (e.g., focussed distraction). What do you think you will notice?

Table 14. Predictions worksheet

When using a short-term behavioural intervention such as abdominal breathing, make prediction a about what you think will occur when you do this. Measure your anxiety level out of 10 (where 10 is the highest it can possibly be) before and after you complete this behaviour.					
Date/time	**Describe behaviour**	**Prediction about what you think will occur when you use this behaviour**	**Anxiety level before using behaviour**	**What actually happened?**	**Anxiety level out of 10 after using behaviour**
6.00pm 12th June	Focussed distraction	Will probably bring my anxiety levels down	7	It was difficult to do it at first as I kept going back to my body. I was eventually able to do it and I started to feel less anxious	3

Table 14. Predictions worksheet

When using a short term behavioural intervention such as abdominal breathing, make prediction a about what you think will occur when you do this. Measure your anxiety level out of 10 (where 10 is the highest it can possibly be) before and after you complete this behaviour.

Date/time	Describe behaviour	Prediction about what you think will occur when you use this behaviour	Anxiety level before using behaviour	What actually happened?	Anxiety level out of 10 after using behaviour

Table 14. Predictions worksheet

When using a short-term behavioural intervention such as abdominal breathing, make prediction a about what you think will occur when you do this. Measure your anxiety level out of 10 (where 10 is the highest it can possibly be) before and after you complete this behaviour.

Date/time	Describe behaviour	Prediction about what you think will occur when you use this behaviour	Anxiety level before using behaviour	What actually happened?	Anxiety level out of 10 after using behaviour

Table 14. Predictions worksheet

When using a short-term behavioural intervention such as abdominal breathing, make prediction a about what you think will occur when you do this. Measure your anxiety level out of 10 (where 10 is the highest it can possibly be) before and after you complete this behaviour.

Date/time	Describe behaviour	Prediction about what you think will occur when you use this behaviour	Anxiety level before using behaviour	What actually happened?	Anxiety level out of 10 after using behaviour

Table 14. Predictions worksheet

When using a short term behavioural intervention such as abdominal breathing, make prediction a about what you think will occur when you do this. Measure your anxiety level out of 10 (where 10 is the highest it can possibly be) before and after you complete this behaviour.

Date/time	Describe behaviour	Prediction about what you think will occur when you use this behaviour	Anxiety level before using behaviour	What actually happened?	Anxiety level out of 10 after using behaviour

Approaching feelings

Melissa B, a teacher, was sitting in front of me. As she spoke she shifted around continuously in her chair, rubbing the back of her neck, grabbing her long red hair, breathing from the top of her chest, sighing and holding her breath at various times. She appeared to be a highly analytical person and was able to articulate her difficulties quite easily. She explained how interpersonal difficulties between herself and work colleagues had started, and she had insight into these problems. However, when I asked her how she was feeling in her body she found it extremely difficult to answer. It wasn't the case that Melissa didn't experience emotions as she was displaying them quite evidently in front of me through her body language. It was more simply a case that Melissa felt very uncomfortable when she recognised her bodily sensations of anxiety and felt a lot more familiar 'remaining or staying put in her head'. When I asked Melissa if she had ever developed any positive coping strategies to soothe herself she couldn't think of any. She stated quite simply that she had been brought up in a household where people didn't talk about their feelings. As a result of this from a very early age Melissa had naturally developed many sophisticated ways of ignoring or controlling her emotions and in fact had become quite an expert in emotional avoidance.

Figure 18 shows an example of the type of relationship that many individuals who experience panic have with their feelings. Generally, painful emotions such as anxiety as well as anger and sadness are viewed as feelings to be feared or to be got rid of. As a result, strategies such as ignoring feelings, distracting the self from feeling feelings, and using safety behaviours to avoid feelings are commonly used. People's natural instinct is to supress uncomfortable feelings in order to feel better. However, an unfortunate consequence of engaging in emotionally avoidant strategies is that emotional distress is maintained at quite a high level or it increases even further over time.

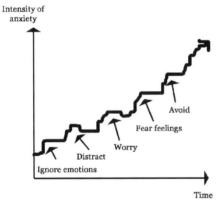

Figure 18. Behaviours that maintain high levels of anxiety

A counter-intuitive solution to panic attacks and anxiety

The ideas covered in the right-hand column of the table on the next page (see table 15) often confuse my clients, because the concepts feel so alien to them. Maybe it's not dissimilar to asking them to grab a red-hot poker, while assuring them that it is not going to harm them. This type of '**counter-intuitive**' strategy to panic is the last thing that most people who experience panic would choose to do as they feel that their anxiety will rise significantly. By the way, when I say counter-intuitive I mean people carrying out behaviours or engaging in thoughts which are the direct opposite of what their intuition or feelings tell them is right.

In my sessions I ask my clients – "What would happen if you tried the opposite of the above? For example, instead of ignoring emotions, you notice them and tell them that it is fine for them to be there?"

"What if instead of distracting yourself from anxiety, you focus on your feelings, and spend time in your body rather than in your head." I also ask – "What would happen if you begin to see anxiety as a friend rather than your enemy, if you allow your anxiety to be visible rather than try to hide it, and give permission for your anxiety to stay, rather than trying to get rid of it as soon as possible?"

Table 15. New strategy for feelings

Commonly applied solutions to anxiety	Strategy based on an opposite approach
Avoid uncomfortable feelings	Approach uncomfortable feelings
Distract self - Keep mind off of feelings	Focus on feelings
Perceive anxiety symptoms as threatening. Fear them	Perceive anxiety as part of the body that works for you. Embrace symptoms and allow symptoms to be visible
Control anxiety, try to get rid of feelings as soon as possible	Allow anxiety to freely move about body.
Tell anxiety that it shouldn't be there	Tell anxiety that that it OK to be there and that it can stay as long as it wants.

An effective wat to approach accepting feelings

If you remind yourself of the ideas covered in the early part of this book, you will remember that the neo-cortex is at the top of the brain, the prefrontal cortex is directly underneath that, and the sub-cortical regions are at the bottom of the brain. A slight problem with people who become highly anxious and panicky is that their pre-frontal cortex tends to go off-line when they are feeling most

distressed. If this happens to you could find yourself in situations, when you are panicking, with your mind going blank, finding it very difficult to think clearly or rationally, and feeling unable to complete CBT exercises.

With this in mind, I suggest that a very useful starting point is to begin viewing yourself as a bit like a <u>parent</u> to the subcortical or primitive regions of the brain. Imagine these parts of the brain not as the enemy, but more like a servant that has worked for you loyally and tirelessly, a servant who is also very rarely appreciated for his or her effort.

"I've got a niggling feeling that Madam's not very happy with me"

The best place to start your new parenting approach will be when you are on your own and when your anxiety levels are mild. Mild anxiety may be around, when you have day-to-day problems, for example, a problem at work, a problem with a friend or a relative etc. Mild distress may also be around when you worry, or when you ask "What if?" questions. The essence of the approach that I am going to suggest you use, is to become more aware of your feelings, especially anxious feelings at the earliest stage possible.

The best way to explain is with a demonstration. This is how a client conversation might develop.

James: "OK, Jemma, I would just like you to think of a problem that you have had just recently, a problem that when you think about it now, still leaves you feeling slightly anxious."

Jemma: "OK, I've thought of something. Do you want me to talk to you about it?"

James: "No, I'd like you to keep it to yourself for now. I'd just like you to think about where you feel your emotions more strongly."

Jemma: "I feel it most in my chest!"

James: "Good. Keep your focus there. Now place one of your hands on your chest in the place where you feel your emotion more strongly. You are placing your hand on your body where your emotion is, because many of us who are prone to avoiding emotions unconsciously and automatically move away from feeling emotions, and go into our heads instead. You are gaining a connection with your emotions and keeping your focus on how you are feeling."

"Placing your hand on the part of your body where you feel your anxiety more strongly will also act as a reminder to you, to keep your focus on your emotions. It is very important while you are doing this exercise to focus on feeling your feelings and

remind yourself that you really are willing for your emotions to be there."

"Focussing on the part of your body underneath you hand with your mind, examine exactly what your emotion feels like. For example, how much space do your feelings take up? How painful or uncomfortable are your feelings. Jemma, can you rate the intensity of your feeling between 1 and 10, where 10 is the highest level of intensity?"

Jemma: "They're about a 7 at the moment."

James: "OK, while you continue to feel your anxiety, mentally give it your permission to take up the space that it is taking up in your body. Taking things a little further I would also like you to speak internally with your anxiety saying something along the lines of the following."

"Thank you for being there" … "There are very good reasons for you being there."

"Keep in mind the idea that from the primitive minds point of view there is a good reason for your anxiety being there, even if it does not make sense logically."

"Now follow that by saying "You are welcome to stay here for as long as you want."

"Bear in mind again Jemma from the primitive mind's point of view that if it notices during its screening process that there is a cue to a potential threat, which may be physical or psychological, it is just doing its job properly if it brings the threat to your attention and helps you to prepare.

The threat does not need to be valid in the current time mode. If it has been perceived as a threat in the past, or you have previously confirmed the existence of the threat by withdrawing from this threat in the past, then from the primitive mind's point of view the threat is still active."

"While feeling your symptoms of anxiety it is important when you speak to your feelings that you really mean what you are saying. Let go of all your thoughts and focus on your feeling. The importance of your self-communication is not in the words that you use but rather your intention behind your words. Keep an idea in mind of accepting, recognising, being grateful, and being patient. I'm just going to ask you to do this for a minute Jemma and we will see what happens."

...a minute passes...

James: "What are you noticing at the moment Jemma?"

Jemma: "The feeling is going down...It's about a 4 now."

James: "OK keep with the feeling, noticing that it is going down. Just stay with it. We'll see what happens in another minute or so."

...another minute passes...

James: "OK, Jemma what are you noticing now?"

Jemma: "It's gone!"

Learning how to stay with your feelings

I'd just like to complete a short recap now. It is important in the early stages of CBT that when you are experiencing anxiety, that you practice being with your feelings as much as possible. This will help you in two ways. Firstly, it will help you to fear your feelings less, and secondly it will make it more likely that you will be able to use your acceptance approach when you are experiencing higher levels of anxiety. You will need to bear in mind that in a state of heightened distress the frontal lobes - *where your self-soothing approach comes from* - stop working somewhat. Practicing acceptance over and over again when you are not so anxious will make it more likely that you will be able to access and use this self-soothing approach automatically when you need it.

The basal ganglia kicks in when we feel distressed

When we become highly anxious we are likely to continue to return to our old unhelpful habitual behaviours due to the strong influence of the basal ganglia which is located in the sub-cortical region of our brain. Activation of the basal ganglia results in us doing the same things that we have always done before. To change the use of unhelpful habits, you will need to practice using your new positive habits - learned through CBT exercises - over and over again. Eventually, your new CBT habits will come into place automatically when you are faced with distressing situations. This process takes time, however, as brain wiring in the basal ganglia does not grow instantly.

Chapter summary

Approaching feelings

- Most individuals who experience panic attacks tend to avoid feeling their anxiety and remain in analytical mode instead.

- Avoiding the processing of emotions tends to keep fear in place and prolongs suffering.

- Counter-intuitive approaches such as focussing on uncomfortable feelings, making room for feelings, and validating anxiety produce positive results in the long-term.

- A useful strategy is to form a positive relationship with the primitive part of the mind.

Chapter 19 - Homework

Using the record sheet (see table 16) to keep a record of your anxiety level before and after you practice making room for your feelings. What do you predict will occur?

Table 16. Accepting emotions record

Use this worksheet to keep a record of your anxiety level before and after you practice making room for your feelings. What do you predict will occur?				
Date/Time	Trigger	Panic level before accepting feelings between 0 and 10 (where 10 is the highest it can be)	Panic level after completing exercise	Observations while completing the exercise
9.00 am 29th June	Heart was racing when I woke up	8	3	Feeling went up and down while I was letting them be there. After about 5 minutes they started to go down.

Table 16. Accepting emotions record

Use this worksheet to keep a record of your anxiety level before and after you practice making room for your feelings. What do you predict will occur?

Date/Time	Trigger	Anxiety level before accepting feelings between 0 and 10 (where 10 is the highest it can be)	Anxiety level after completing exercise	Observations while completing the exercise

Table 16. Accepting emotions record

Use this worksheet to keep a record of your anxiety level before and after you practice making room for your feelings. What do you predict will occur?

Date/Time	Trigger	Anxiety level before accepting feelings between 0 and 10 (where 10 is the highest it can be)	Anxiety level after completing exercise	Observations while completing the exercise

Table 16. Accepting emotions record

Use this worksheet to keep a record of your anxiety level before and after you practice making room for your feelings. What do you predict will occur?

Date/Time	Trigger	Anxiety level before accepting feelings between 0 and 10 (where 10 is the highest it can be)	Anxiety level after completing exercise	Observations while completing the exercise

Table 16. Accepting emotions record

Use this worksheet to keep a record of your anxiety level before and after you practice making room for your feelings. What do you predict will occur?

Date/Time	Trigger	Anxiety level before accepting feelings between 0 and 10 (where 10 is the highest it can be)	Anxiety level after completing exercise	Observations while completing the exercise

How to respond to distressing thoughts

As I suggested in the previous chapter a key to teaching yourself how to reduce symptoms of panic is the relationship that you develop with your anxious feelings. Once panic is activated a cocktail of hormones is released into your blood stream and these hormones will need time to work their way through your body.

Problems can occur if we react to fear in an avoidant, critical, controlling, or angry way. Clinical experience tells me that the sub-cortical mind – or primitive part of the self - does not react well to being controlled, but it does react much more favourably to being noticed, to being thanked, to being treated non-judgementally, welcomed, and soothed. In essence, a more adaptive strategy is to move away from a controlling approach and move towards self-regulation and containment. You will need to work on gaining the trust of the primitive part of the self. When that occurs the primitive part of the self will be more willing for your rational mind to take charge. This is not unlike gaining the trust from a frightened animal. An analogy that I often use to describe this in sessions, is imagining the mind like a horse and a rider. The rider being the neo-cortex and the horse the primitive brain. The rider communicates with the horse by listening, acknowledging, and validating.

If during symptoms of panic you hear an internal voice stating "I'm having a heart attack" it is important to hear what is being said, to make a mental note of it or to even write it down.

Here follows a hypothetical communication between the neo-cortex and the primitive brain system.

Primitive brain – "Something's badly wrong."

Neo-cortex – "What's happening? What's going on? What's wrong?"

Primitive brain – "I'm having a heart attack."

Neo-cortex – "OK, I am going to focus on the feeling. I am noticing that your heart is beating really fast, you're breathing much faster than usual, you're trembling and you feel really frightened."

Primitive brain – "Is this the end?"

Neo-cortex – "That really is a very frightening thought."

Primitive brain – "Do something quickly. I can't breathe."

Neo-cortex – "You're really frightened at the moment, I know that feels really uncomfortable, these feelings are there because you're experiencing panic. I am going to help you to focus on feeling these feelings and to help you to allow these feelings to be there. You will continue to feel frightened and very uncomfortable for a little while because adrenaline is still pumping through your system. It will soon work its way through, when you don't fight it. Allow yourself to breath more slowly and more deeply.

Primitive brain – "Think it's OK now."

The above dialogue sounds slightly artificial but it gives a sense of the type of compassionate communication that we are aiming for. To reduce your symptoms of panic you will need to train your neo-cortex to be compassionate, to listen, to validate, and to form a positive relationship with the primitive part of your mind. This approach will generally offer a soothing or dampening presence to the primitive part of the mind.

For some people the idea of talking kindly to what for a long time has been viewed as 'the enemy' seems remarkably farfetched. When starting to use this new approach you may need to internally engage with it in an 'as if' capacity. Even if you start by actively pretending, the intention to behave differently, i.e., with compassion and caring will begin to evolve into a more natural and authentic process for you.

Chapter summary

How to respond to distressing thoughts

- Problems can occur if we react to frightening thoughts in a critical, controlling, or angry way.

- Good communication by the neo-cortex with the primitive part of the brain involves listening and validating feelings/sensations.

- Training the neo-cortex to be compassionate and to listen will help you form a positive relationship with the primitive part of the mind.

How worry and rumination make things worse

Most people who experience panic symptoms will spend a significant portion of their time worrying or ruminating. Because these processes tend to maintain emotional difficulties it is important that we take a look at them.

Rumination is a process of churning negative thoughts over in one's mind. Most ruminative thoughts are connected to the self and the past. Some people suggest that rumination is useful because it can help to create lots of possibilities, and can offer solutions when we are faced with specific problems.

Rumination, however, does not work well when we try to analyse our way out of emotional distress.

A process of rumination is kept in place by the questions we ask ourselves. For example, if we ask "Why does this keep happening to me" or "What's wrong with me?" The questions that we ask ourselves throw up answers which, in turn, can lead us to ask more questions. Before long, if this process continues unstopped we can end up confirming our worst fears, for example, that we are worthless, wrong, useless, bad, and such like. The irony of the whole process is that in our search for ways to avoid current or future painful feelings by ruminating, we end up dwelling on the past and we can end up feeling worse than ever. It's not dissimilar to using a shovel to dig ourselves out of a hole. The more we dig, the deeper the hole gets! The problem is that often we do not feel that we have any other way of solving our problems, so we continue to use the same strategy, even though we know it does not work. I'll just give a hypothetical example now about how a conversation might go between a CBT therapist and a client.

CLIENT - "What's the difference between worry and rumination?"

CBT THERAPIST - "Worry and rumination are similar in that they both involve thought churning. The main difference between them is that worry is focussed on the future and being able to cope with potential outcomes, whereas rumination is focussed on the past."

"When people worry they think about upcoming situations and ask questions such as "What will I do if this happens?" "What is the worst thing that could happen?" or "What if this happens?" They do this because they think that if they can imagine the worst case scenario, then they will be able to put things in place to deal with whatever happens in a particular situation. They think if they can work out what might happen in advance then they will be safe. Ironically, however, just like rumination, in an attempt to achieve certainty and to feel safe, we can end up feeling more frightened than ever, and also experience intrusive thoughts."

CLIENT - "Intrusive thoughts?"

CBT THERAPIST – "An intrusive thought is a thought that pushes its way into awareness with extreme urgency. Intrusive thoughts often appear to come out of nowhere and carry high levels of emotional distress with them. Ironically, intrusive thoughts alone can trigger panic."

"Before I explain why intrusive thoughts may occur, I want to offer you a simple analogy about the functioning of the mind."

"First I'd like you to recognise that they have a **conscious mind.** When people use their conscious minds they are awake to thoughts, images or sensations that they experience. I'd like us to imagine that the conscious mind is a bit like a magic white board that begins to erase what is written on it after only a few seconds. Because the ink or information expressed using the ink disappears so rapidly the only way to keep anything live on this white board is to continuously write on it over and over again. When new information is written on the white board, information that was on the white board previously, disappears even more rapidly. A further point to note is that the amount of information that can be written on the whiteboard at any one point in time is limited due to the whiteboards small size."

CLIENT - "So you saying the mind is like a white-board. I'm not sure I understand?"

CBT THERAPIST - "Do you mind if I demonstrate with you? It's much easier to show you how this works rather than to explain it. Before we start I just want to let you know that this is not a test. It's just a little exercise so that you can find out how much information your mind can hold onto. I am going to start by asking you to remember five random numbers and letters. Are you ready?

CLIENT - "Yes"

CBT THERAPIST - "5A3KQ. Have you got that?"

CLIENT - "Yes. I think so!"

CBT THERAPIST – "Alright I now want you to remember these numbers as well."

"27KR1...Right, can you repeat that sequence for me?"

CLIENT - "27KR1"

CBT THERAPIST - "Good...And, the first sequence"

CLIENT - "...Erm ... [a big pause follows] ...57...Q...It seems to have gone out of my head... I'm sorry."

CBT THERAPIST - "There's no need to be sorry. This is exactly what is meant to happen. This is how the mind works. We just gave your internal whiteboard an impossible task. Hardly anyone can recall over 9 randomly presented units of information unless they use specialised memory techniques, and I just gave you 10. That's why I'm saying the whiteboard is small."

"I'll just explain it a bit more. A benefit of the white board's disappearing ink process is that it is constantly available for continuous use. As a result of this, huge amounts of information can be written on the whiteboard during the period of its lifetime. In many respects, it could be suggested that we could feel grateful that the whiteboard loses access to information so quickly. If it didn't it would quite quickly become jammed up with too much information and become unusable."

"Taking this idea further, I'd like us to imagine that our **out of conscious processes** work a little bit like a building that the white board is housed in. I'll just explain that out of conscious processes are brain functions that we are unaware of, or mental processes that go on in the back of our minds."

CLIENT - "And, what's the significance of associating the out of conscious mind with a building?"

CBT THERAPIST - "I'm saying that out of conscious processes are like a building because the amount of brain space required for out of conscious thinking is absolutely huge in in comparison to the amount of brain used for the white board. The building is also three dimensional unlike the two dimensional whiteboard, there are also multiple rooms, and secret passageways.

CLIENT - "I understand why it is big but what does the three dimensional layout of the building represent, with multiple rooms and such like?"

CBT THERAPIST - "This represents an idea that the out of conscious mind can think on several different levels at the same time. It can absorb information from our environment, take care of all of our bodily functions, plan our activities, assist our communication, and think about problems we have in our lives without us being aware of it. It can also use symbols, images, and words to create ideas and connect them up in a way that we would struggle to do consciously. What it can do is really quite incredible!"

"In this building there are also filing cabinets crammed with information that we thought we had forgotten about, and there are reams of papers lying around waiting to be filed."

CLIENT - "What do the reams of papers represent?"

CBT THERAPIST - "The reams of paper represent thoughts that we have not fully processed or ideas that we are currently working on. Many people may have several hundred or even thousands of different thoughts strands they are working on at any one time. Thought strands may be about relationships with different people, hobbies or interests, work projects, holidays and such like. Information does not disappear easily from this building but very often it can get lost or misfiled."

CLIENT - "So how does it get lost or misfiled?"

CBT THERAPIST - "There is so much information in this building or in peoples' minds that sometimes it is hard for them to find what they are looking for. The more information that's in the building the harder it is to find what they need."

"Now imagine that in this building there is a little librarian who is very loyal to you and will try to find answers to anything that you ask using the whiteboard, even if it means working through the night. Sometimes the librarian finds information quickly, sometimes it might take days, but when the librarian finds answers to questions posed on the whiteboard it will post it an answer on the whiteboard just as soon as space becomes available."

CLIENT - "I'm still not sure I still fully understand this analogy of a librarian. How does this work with real problems?"

CBT THERAPIST - "OK. Let's imagine that you are walking down the street one day and on the other side of the street there is a girl whose face you recognise. You are immediately aware that you know her but this is not where you usually see her. You ask yourself "Where do I know her from?" a few times. Nothing comes to her mind immediately and you carry on doing whatever you were doing before. You may even forget that you asked that question as it disappears from your conscious awareness and it is replaced by other things. However, a little while later, maybe a few hours, days, or sometimes weeks later, an idea pops into your mind telling you where you knew the person you saw in the street from. How do you think this might happen?"

CLIENT - "Well I guess the little librarian had not forgotten that I asked that question, perhaps she was going through the filing cabinets looking for an answer or maybe she waited for me to go somewhere and suddenly remembered."

CBT THERAPIST - "That's what I'm saying. As soon as an opportunity occurred and there was space available on the whiteboard the librarian posted the information. A useful rule of thumb, therefore, will be to assume that when we ask our brain a question it will continue to work on questions posed to it even though we may have consciously forgotten that we have asked the questions in the first place."

"Usually the little librarian will put thoughts or information in a queue to enter conscious awareness, and in this respect answers to questions you have asked will wait patiently to pop into your mind when there is space available or when the mind is not occupied with something else."

CLIENT - "Is that why so many thoughts go through my head at night just as I want to go to sleep?"

CBT THERAPIST - "Yes, that what I'm getting at. You will have access to these thoughts at night because your mind is not focussed on other things."

CLIENT - "What about the other thoughts you mentioned earlier. I think you said they were intrusive thoughts. I used to get those a lot?"

CBT THERAPIST - "Intrusive thoughts are different to the above mentioned patient type of thoughts that we have. They are not dissimilar to the librarian pushing through a registered letter for your attention. Intrusive thoughts are pushed through to consciousness, as a priority, pushing out any other information that is currently on line. You may be talking with someone when one of these thoughts pops into your head. For example, if you are socially anxious, an image of yourself looking odd could suddenly be pushed into your mind. Intrusive thoughts are sent with high degrees of importance and you will notice them as a result of the emotional intensity that comes with them."

157

CLIENT - "So where do they come from?"

CBT THERAPIST – "There may be many factors responsible for the creation of intrusive thoughts. One way that they may be generated is by worrying or asking "What if?" questions. This type of questioning process certainly appears to increase the likelihood of intrusive thoughts being pushed into consciousness. It is important to recognise than that when we receive intrusive thought messages they are not 'evidence' for anything. Although intrusive thoughts often feel uncomfortable, because they bring fear with them, it does not make these thoughts any more real than any other thoughts that pop into your mind."

"I think the best way to explain this is by talking about a young man I worked with a little while ago."

"Gregory was a big worrier. He would often go through a process of worry, asking "What if?" questions to his mind and his brain would usually send him back the worst possible things that could happen, or what could go wrong. His intentions for worrying were positive as he felt that this type of questioning process could keep him safe. He thought that if he knew about the types of problems that might occur in advance then he could be prepared for them. Before going to the cinema with friends Gregory would ask himself about what could go wrong. His obedient mind usually sent him answers. One type of answer generated and sent to his conscious awareness was that he may end up in a middle seat feeling panicky, with everyone around noticing him, and he would feel humiliated."

CLIENT - "I think most people would be anxious about that, wouldn't they?"

CBT THERAPIST - "They might do if they worried a lot about what people thought about them. But remember nothing had *actually* happened at this point. This was all in his mind. But, based on the ideas that his mind gave him Gregory decided to take action and sit at the back near an aisle seat so that he could make a quick exit if required. Gregory then began to think of how he could position himself in an aisle seat. He thought that if he could go in first in his group of friends he could stand near an aisle seat and gesture to others to go in ahead of him. His mind came up with a further ideas, such as if anyone questioned his need to sit in an aisle seat, he would say that he had a stomach ache and may need to go to the bathroom. He also had thoughts about phoning his friends up at the last minute and telling them that he couldn't make it. The amount of worrying that Gregory experienced before going to the cinema made the whole process of going to the cinema a difficult experience rather than the enjoyable experience that it could have been. Gregory's mind also reminded him how strange he was for engaging in this type of behaviour, and his friends would never think that he was like that."

CLIENT - "So what happened to him?"

CBT THERAPIST - "A big risk for Gregory was deciding not to ask "What if?" questions. A big part of Gregory thought that asking himself these questions kept him prepared, safe and not vulnerable. Recognising that all thoughts that come into awareness are simply offerings sent by the mind and not ideas supported by evidence made a significant difference to Gregory. Gregory learnt how to stand back and observe his thoughts, and recognise that any thought that came into awareness was just a suggestion. Just because he had a thought did not mean it needed to be dealt with. As such, learning to notice his thoughts made a significant difference to him."

"Many people's minds come up with all sorts of negative ideas when they worry. In Gregory's case a worry for him was losing control, being thought of by others as weak, and others thinking that there was something wrong with him. I drew a diagram on my office whiteboard for Gregory to look at. I have copied this onto the next page. It's a little bit similar to the diagrams that Christine Padesky uses."

CLIENT - "Isn't she one of the authors of the book 'Mind over Mood?"

CBT THERAPIST - "That right! Christine Padesky's ideas are very useful to us here to explain what was happening to Gregory. Gregory engaged in numerous avoidant type behaviours which tended to confirm his fear based thoughts still further. By carrying out avoidant behaviours Gregory did not collect alternative evidence that challenged his fears."

CBT THERAPIST - "Gregory's example shows how the interactions between thoughts, feelings and behaviour have a tendency to maintain problems. In this case, interfering with Gregory's worry processes led to him having less frightening thoughts, which in turn led to a reduction in his tendency to want to avoid situations."

Research

Intrusive thoughts are defined as unwanted thoughts images or impulses. In 2014 Richard Moulding & his colleagues completed an international study to identify a) the prevalence of intrusive thoughts and b) how people react to them. They assessed 777 students across 15 cities, 13 countries, and 6 continents. They found that 93 percent of their students experienced intrusive thoughts in the previous 3 months, suggesting that intrusive thoughts are in fact a normal part of daily living. The researchers' natural conclusion was therefore - It is not the intrusive thoughts themselves that maintain mental health problems, but rather it is how we react to them.

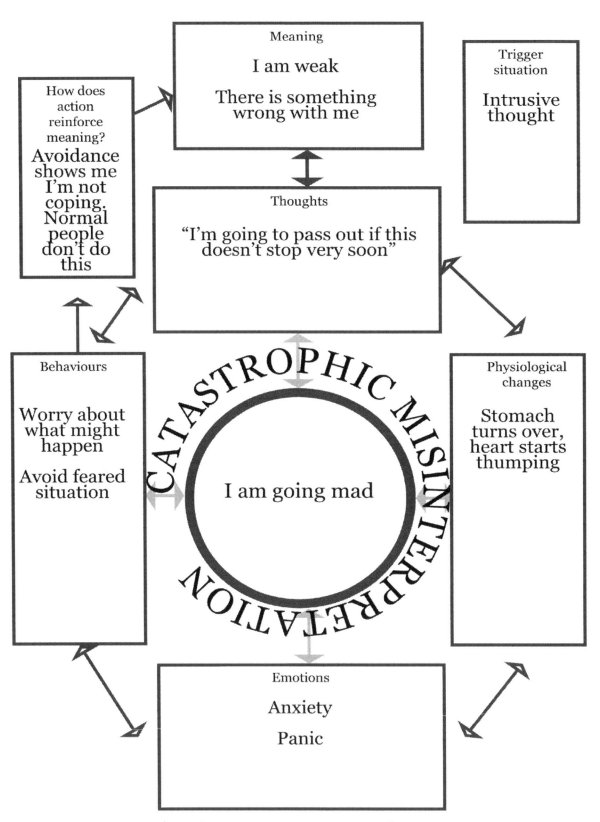

Figure 19. Gregory's example

Chapter summary

How worry and rumination make things worse

- Worry does not happen by itself. It is a safety mechanism that many of us use to help us feel prepared for upcoming situations.

- The frequency of intrusive thoughts about panic are increased by the worry process.

- Intrusive thoughts, although frightening are no more fact-based that any other thought.

- The emotional impact of thoughts can be reduced by noticing them rather than reacting to them.

- Avoiding situations as a result of reacting to intrusive thoughts can lead to problems being maintained.

Retraining the sub-cortical mind

As many of us are aware, when we worry about the potential outcomes of panic, reassuring ourselves appears to have a limited impact. You may well have read the contents of this book and hopefully by now have more knowledge about panic symptoms. However, despite this you may continue to experience intense feelings of anxiety in various situations. If you are at this stage, your neo-cortex understands panic, but the primitive brain has yet to take on board the same information.

With this in mind one of the most helpful ways to teach the primitive mind how to absorb new information is through experience. I will explain using an analogy.

I would like to invite you to think of the primitive mind as a child who comes to your bedroom door one night feeling frightened. You ask the child what she is frightened of and she says that she thinks there is something – a monster - in her wardrobe. You have several options in terms of your response.

- You could tell the child not to be so silly and completely ignore her. The result of this is that that the child waits around outside your room and continues to try to gain your attention. She could even wait outside your bedroom door for the whole night.
- You could rationalise with the child. You explain to her how impossible it is that a monster could get into her wardrobe and that monsters don't exist. You tell her that she is thinking about monsters because she watched a frightening television programme about monsters earlier. The result of this is that the child nods while listening and goes back to her room for a short while, but is back outside your room a few minutes later.
- You could tell the child that she can sleep in a put-down bed in your room. The child is not scared anymore and happily gets into this bed. However, when the next day comes she seems more terrified than before of sleeping in her bedroom.

Or

- You could take the child's hand acknowledging that she feels really frightened and tell her that you are both going to look into the wardrobe together. When you approach the wardrobe the child is really scared and she tries to resist going towards the wardrobe.

You gently persist telling the child that it really is OK to feel frightened. When you have opened the wardrobe door and you both have had a good look inside for a couple of minutes you notice that the child has become a lot less anxious and is happier once more to sleep in her own bed. You don't hear any more from the child until you see her the next morning.

With the fourth option you don't have to explain or rationalise, you simply help the child to acknowledge that she is scared. You take her to the situation which you know logically is very low risk (i.e., there is a very low probability of there being a monster in her wardrobe) and encourage her to find out for herself how dangerous the situation is. The child learns by her own experience.

There is one more thing to note in this area. The child looking in the wardrobe will need to do this without carrying out any ritualistic behaviours or safety mechanisms. These could include crossing fingers, closing her eyes, holding onto a teddy bear etc. If the child uses these things for reassurance then the child will believe that her safety behaviours are keeping her safe and she will continue to need them. Remember many people who experience panic attacks have safety behaviours, such as carrying diazepam, using beta-blockers, worrying, distracting the self by listening to music etc.

In the next chapter we will look at eliminating safety behaviours using a route of least resistance.

Chapter summary

Retraining the sub-cortical mind

- The sub-cortical mind does not update its self automatically as you acquire new knowledge.

- The sub-cortical mind learns through direct experience. It needs to be shown that things are OK, rather than being told that things are OK.

An easy way to reprogram the sub-cortical mind

23

As I mentioned in earlier chapters, for many of us there is a distinct journey that our panic attacks have taken. Your first panic attack was an undoubted surprise. It came out of the blue possibly connected to high overall stress levels. Following this you may have tried to make sense of your experience without access to accurate information about panic. This may have led to many distressing thoughts about various potential scenarios. You may have begun to fear your own feelings and began to look for cues that triggered feelings of anxiety such as your own physiological reactions. You may have gradually started to reduce your access to situations that triggered anxiety to bring down your overall distress levels. You could then have noticed a gradual erosion of your self-esteem and confidence. Following this you could have searched for external sources of help such as medication.

Starting to take charge of your life

Some or all of the above may be relevant to you in your situation, but the starting point of taking charge of your life will be to desensitise yourself to your own fear reactions. To do this you will need to write down all of the a) situations that you have been avoiding and b) safety behaviours that you currently fear dropping. You will then need to grade each item on your list in terms of the level of anxiety you will experience when either approaching a feared situation or dropping a safety behaviour. Rate the most frightening item on your list as a ten and then compare each other situation to it giving each item on your list an anxiety score out of ten. Paul's list is shown below. The situation that provoked the most anxiety for Paul was going on an aeroplane, so Paul recorded this behaviour as a 10. Each other item on Paul's list was compared against this.

Paul's list

Make room and accept feelings when feeling slightly anxious (1)

Attend psychology appointment without partner (3)

In session raise heart rate by completing gentle exercise (5)

Tell a friend about my panic attacks (5.5)

In session breathe out rapidly to expel carbon dioxide which leads to dizzy feeling in the head. Do I faint? (6)

Do not use anti-anxiety medication before carrying out anxiety evoking activities (7)

Do not carry anti-anxiety medication just in case (7.5)

Deliberately sit in the middle of a row of seats in a cinema/theatre (8)

Don't go to the toilet just before I go out (related to fear of losing control of bowels) (8)

Be a passenger in a car rather than the driver (short trip non-motorway) (8.5)

Drive on a motorway rather than a country road (short trip) (9)

Drive on motorway (long trip) (9.5)

Passenger in an uncrowded tube (related to fear of losing control) (9.5)

Passenger in a crowded tube (10)

Passenger in an aeroplane (short haul) (10)

Once you have completed your list you will then need to work your way through it starting with the behaviours that provoke the lowest level of anxiety. It is very important that for anything you engage with on your list you accept your feelings while doing it, (see the chapter on processing emotions).

You will also need to be mindful that when completing items on your list you do this without using any additional safety behaviours, such as holding your breath, distracting yourself, etc. Do not move onto higher anxiety evoking situations on your list until your anxiety about completing things lower down on your list has reduced significantly or is easily tolerated.

If you find that your anxiety does not reduce, don't persist with this approach. It might be that there are earlier emotionally unprocessed memories or traumatic experiences that need attention or working through. Unprocessed memories or traumas can often be a contributory factor to anticipatory anxiety in the present time mode. If this is the case, I recommend that that you don't try to work on these memories on your own. You will be better off working with a trained therapist.

Paul's experience

Initially when Paul left to attend his psychology session without his partner his anxiety rose to quite a high level. He was able to make room for his feelings, giving permission for himself to feel anxious while carrying out this new behaviour. As you might imagine after Paul attended his psychology session alone for the first time the primitive part of his brain discovered that nothing actually happened and it altered the threat level for him attending future appointments alone. Following this Paul's anxiety about attending appointments by himself reduced significantly and he attended all of his future appointments alone. Paul also reported that other items on his list seemed far more achievable than he previously thought and did not create as much anxiety as he initially anticipated. As he progressed through his list Paul noted that in general terms his mood had improved and that he felt more confident.

It is important to note that each individual fear can be broken down into much smaller units. For example, approaching a tube could be broken down into numerous other little challenges (see table 18). Each of these challenges can be further broken down into even smaller challenges (see table 19), and so on.

Using exposure sheets

Exposure is part of a process of desensitisation. When you use desensitisation you will need to stay in anxiety provoking situations until your anxiety is very easy to tolerate. To assist with your learning process you could assess your anxiety level before, during, and after the situation you place yourself in or while you are using a new behaviour, (see table 20). After you have completed your exposure work think to yourself about what you have learnt from your experience. This will further embed your experiential learning, (learning by doing/experiencing). I have placed a thumbnail of a typical exposure sheet below. A larger version of this form can be found at the end of this chapter.

Table 20. Exposure sheet

Time, date	Situation	Anxiety before (0 - 10 where 10 is max)	Anxiety during (0 - 10 where 10 is max)	Anxiety after (0 - 10 where 10 is max)	What did I learn?

Table 18. Systematic desensitisation sheet

Overall target situation, object, or behaviour for desensitisation

Go on a tube in London

Individual target area for desensitisation	Predicted distress level 0 to 10
Go into foyer of tube station. Stay there until distress reduces to zero and then exit tube station.	2
Go down long escalator and back up to surface again.	3
Use lift	6
Go on overland train accompanied by someone.	7
Go on overland train alone	8
Go on tube accompanied by therapist	8
Go on tube accompanied by friend	9
Go on tube alone	10

Table 19. Systematic desensitisation sheet

Overall target situation, object, or behaviour for desensitisation

Use lift as part of desensitisation process of going on a tube in London.

Individual target area for desensitisation	Predicted distress level 0 to 10
Go to lift (not used much) with therapist	1
Go in lift with doors open and get out again (with therapist)	2
Go in lift with doors kept open and get out again (without therapist)	3
Go in lift with doors kept open and get out again (without therapist)	4
Go in lift, let doors close and then open. Then get out again without therapist	5
Go in lift let doors close and open, go down or up one floor and get out again (with therapist)	5
Go in lift let doors close and open, go down or up one floor and get out again (without therapist)	6
Go in lift let doors close and open, go down or up two floors and get out again (without therapist)	6

Table 19. Systematic desensitisation sheet

Overall target situation, object, or behaviour for desensitisation

Individual target area for desensitisation	Predicted distress level 0 to 10

Table 20. Exposure sheet

Time/date	Situation	Anxiety before (0 - 10 where 10 is max)	Anxiety during (0 - 10 where 10 is max)	Anxiety after (0 - 10 where 10 is max)	What did I learn?

Table 19. Systematic desensitisation sheet

Overall target situation, object, or behaviour for desensitisation

Individual target area for desensitisation	Predicted distress level 0 to 10

Table 20. Exposure sheet

Time/date	Situation	Anxiety before (0 - 10 where 10 is max)	Anxiety during (0 - 10 where 10 is max)	Anxiety after (0 - 10 where 10 is max)	What did I learn?

Table 19. Systematic desensitisation sheet

Overall target situation, object, or behaviour for desensitisation

Individual target area for desensitisation	Predicted distress level 0 to 10

Table 20. Exposure sheet

Time/date	Situation	Anxiety before (0 – 10 where 10 is max)	Anxiety during (0 - 10 where 10 is max)	Anxiety after (0 - 10 where 10 is max)	What did I learn?

Table 19. Systematic desensitisation sheet

Overall target situation, object, or behaviour for desensitisation

Individual target area for desensitisation	Predicted distress level 0 to 10

Table 20. Exposure sheet

Time/date	Situation	Anxiety before (0 - 10 where 10 is max)	Anxiety during (0 - 10 where 10 is max)	Anxiety after (0 - 10 where 10 is max)	What did I learn?

Table 19. Systematic desensitisation sheet

Overall target situation, object, or behaviour for desensitisation

Individual target area for desensitisation	Predicted distress level 0 to 10

Table 20. Exposure sheet

Time/date	Situation	Anxiety before (0 - 10 where 10 is max)	Anxiety during (0 - 10 where 10 is max)	Anxiety after (0 - 10 where 10 is max)	What did I learn?

Chapter summary

An easy way to reprogram the threat perception centre

- To desensitise yourself to your feelings of anxiety make a list of all of the things that you have been avoiding.

- Gradually work your way through the list approaching the item which evokes the least anxiety first making room for your feelings at all times.

Behavioural experiments with panic

Behavioural experiments can be very helpful in challenging the thoughts that drive panic. The general idea behind them is to teach the self to learn positive behaviour change through breaking patterns of old unhelpful behaviour. To carry out a behavioural experiment you will need to make a decision to change a behaviour and then put yourself directly in a position to make that behaviour change happen. You will need to make a prediction before the behaviour is carried out, (what you think or feel might happen). When you carry out the behaviour it is important that you record the results. The majority of us make assumptions about a) how others might react to our behaviour, or b) how we might feel if we carry out a certain behaviour. A lot of the time, however, our assumptions are based on inaccurate information or indeed a lack of knowledge. Behavioural experiments help with the development of experiential knowledge.

Completing a behavioural experiment will involve you making a prediction about what you think may occur if you change your behaviour in a particular situation. After you have made a prediction, you will then carry out your new behaviour and observe what occurs.

In my clinical practice I regularly carry out behavioural experiments with my clients. Typically, behavioural experiments can be used to challenge catastrophic misinterpretations in panic, such as I'm going to faint, I'm going to fall over, I'm going to lose control etc. I have placed an example of a typical behavioural experiment on the next page (see table 21.)

Table 21. Behavioural experiment sheet

Describe old behaviour or safety behaviour.
   Sitting down when I feel dizzy or light-headed

Describe new behaviour.
   Remain standing when I feel dizzy. Allow the feeling to pass.

How will you carry out new behaviour?

   I will deliberately make myself feel dizzy, perhaps by spinning myself around quite quickly.
   I will then stay standing and wait to see what actually happens.

Predictions about what will happen when you drop the safety behaviour. Write down as many scenarios as possible.

   I will fall over. I will faint or pass out.

Carry out new behaviour and write down what actually happened here.

   I made myself feel dizzy. It felt uncomfortable initially, because of the light-headedness, but I didn't fall over or faint, and the dizziness gradually passed by itself.

What did you learn from this process?
How likely are you to carry out this new behaviour again?

   I don't need to feel so frightened of feeling dizzy. I could definitely do it again.

Table 21. Behavioural experiment sheet

Describe old behaviour or safety behaviour.

Describe new behaviour.

How will you carry out new behaviour?

Predictions about what will happen when you drop the safety behaviour. Write down as many scenarios as possible.

Carry out new behaviour and write down what actually happened here.

What did you learn from this process?
How likely are you to carry out this new behaviour again?

Chapter summary

Behavioural experiments with panic

- Behavioural experiments are very helpful for challenging catastrophic misinterpretations.

- Completing a behavioural experiment involves you making a prediction about what you think is going to occur, doing it, and then finding out what actually happens.

What did you make of that?

A process that you can use as you reprogram the primitive part of your brain and to further embed the results of your new experiences is to ask yourself what you have learnt.

A reflective process brings more useful thoughts to the front of your mind and into conscious awareness. I will give an example from Melissa once more. Initially, when the model of approaching anxiety was covered with her, Melissa was slightly hesitant about applying it. Her prediction was that her anxiety would at best say the same or it would become more intense. After initially producing some anxiety artificially by engaging in worrying thoughts Melissa then began to practice making room for and accepting her feelings.

Melissa reported that her symptoms of anxiety were initially a 7 out of 10, (where 10 would be the most intense her anxiety could be). After one minute of focussing on her feelings and accepting them she found that her anxiety had reduced to a 5. After two minutes her anxiety had reduced to a 2. When the exercise was complete Melissa felt quite shocked at the results. She had never imagined that this type of approach would reduce her symptoms of anxiety.

Equally in another session Derek and I challenged his fear that he might faint when his mind felt dizzy. We created a dizzy feeling by artificially creating a process of hyperventilation and asking him to stand up while doing this. Dereck soon became less anxious when he realised that he did not faint when he was feeling light-headed and that he could do this for as long as he wanted.

A reflective process after completing this exercise helped Dereck bring new more accurate ideas to his awareness. Through reflection he recognised that

- The counter-intuitive approach worked in his session at least.
- That what he thought would happen did not happen.
- That by trying something new he felt a sense of hope
- That it was highly likely that the same approach would work outside of sessions also.

It was important to help Dereck reflect on this process as much as possible because the brain does not automatically review and revise. In fact, it seems that it can continue to repeat patterns of behaviour, even when behaviours are outdated or no longer work effectively.

Chapter summary

What did you make of that?

- Asking reflective questions stimulates cognitive processes that can aid your learning experience.

- Bringing ideas into awareness such as what you thought might happen, what actually happened, and what you learnt will give you an opportunity to challenge thoughts that lie in the background of your mind creating a negative influence.

- Reflective processes encourage the brain to review and revise outdated, inefficient, and inaccurate thinking processes.

How to prevent relapse

26

In the earlier years of our practice we noticed that after an average of about three to five years about 10% of clients returned to us with their original panic symptoms once more. These particular clients reported that after their period of treatment was complete they felt much happier and as a result didn't need to use the techniques they learnt as much. Over time it seemed that our clients slowly forgot how to use them. As a result of this over a period of years they gradually retracted back to their original position.

Working with these individuals for a second time usually involved just a few sessions and generally much less treatment was required compared to when they initially came to us. They were able to quickly relearn the strategies that they used before and found it much easier to put change processes into place on their return to therapy. There was much less fear about using a process of accepting feelings and engaging in systematic desensitisation as these individuals were able to access useful evidence from their past experiences.

To reduce relapse problems with our clients we began to use an idea that we referred to as the 'Law of Opposites' (Ridgeway & Manning, 2008). With this approach, at the end of treatment we would ask our clients to think about all the ideas that they might forget about or the behaviours that they could once again employ if they wanted to return to their original pre-therapy position. We encouraged our clients to make their list as exhaustive as possible. When our clients list was

Table 22 Law of opposites approach

Previous approach	New approach
Avoid uncomfortable feelings.	Approach uncomfortable feelings.
Distract self – Keep mind off of feelings.	Focus on feelings.
Perceive anxiety symptoms as threatening. Try to escape from them.	Perceive anxiety as part of the body that is trying to help me. Embrace symptoms.
Control anxiety, try to extinguish symptoms as soon as possible.	Allow emotions to be in my body for as long as they need to be there.
Worry about potential problems that may occur so that solutions can be applied.	Drop pre-planning before going into situations that are associated with panic symptoms.
Use safety behaviours, such as using country roads, pre-driving routes.	Drop safety behaviours. If I notice that I am using avoidance, approach problems instead.

was complete we asked them to think of solutions to each point on their list.

Paul's list is shown in the left-hand column (see table 22). The main aspect that Paul noticed on reflection was that he was more aware of his body's reactions to situations after therapy. Instead of interpreting signs of anxiety as an indication that something bad was going to happen to him, he now recognised that his body was creating a preparatory response. When he viewed his anxiety in this way he no longer felt as though anxiety was his enemy and when he approached new situations he took his anxiety with him. Generally, he noticed that his anxiety only rose in the early stages, but as soon as he embraced it and he stayed in any particular situation it soon dissipated.

A useful idea is to get your list out on a regular basis to assess if there is any slippage back to your previous way of approaching your symptoms. Keeping a log that documents your journey with panic or anxiety may also prove useful. You will then be able to look back over this log at a future point in time if you need to quickly revise or recap on approaches that worked for you.

Chapter summary

How to prevent relapse

- If you discontinue using the techniques learnt in this book there is an increased likelihood of relapse.

- Become aware of the risk factors involved in relapse by using the "Law of Opposites" exercise.

- Regularly look at your risk factors and if you notice any slippage back to your old positon then put your counter-intuitive strategies in place.

- Keep a log of your experiences. Reflect on the result of positive changes.

Other therapies for panic attacks

Although CBT is one of the best treatments for panic attacks, many other treatments can also be very beneficial.

Medication

Medication is still the most commonly used treatment for anxiety and evidence indicates that a combination of CBT and medication is more beneficial than using either approach alone. There are logical reasons that explain why medication enhances a CBT approach. If at a biological level the mind does not have the capacity to think straight there is very little likelihood that people will have the concentration or energy to complete CBT exercise effectively, or to make any of the changes I have covered in this book. Medication may give people the extra energy or boost required to make these changes. Equally, if you take medication without making any changes to your behaviour you will not be making the best use of your medication.

Many people who experience panic attacks can start to withdraw from activities and social events that they previously enjoyed, which can also lead to symptoms of depression. Medication can help people to lift out of an anxious position and when this happens they once again feel able to resume normal activities which can lift them back into a positive mood state. In this respect medication can be viewed as a pick-me-up that helps people carry on down their path once more. Medication does not, however, resolve the issue of what makes a panic attack occur in the first place.

Mindfulness

Growing evidence indicates that mindfulness can be very helpful for people who experience all types of mental health problems. In my experience it tends to work because it

- Encourages processing and observation of feelings.
- Helps people to stay in the present moment and detach from ruminative thinking and worrying.
- Exercises the pre-frontal cortex which then becomes more effective at 1) reducing background noise in the mind, and 2) regulating emotions.

As with the use of CBT exercises you will need to keep using mindfulness based approaches in order to maintain your positive mood state. Being mindful will also help you become much more aware of the types of environment and people that impact on your mood state. With awareness comes choice. You can choose to move away from negative environments and negative people if you wish. Equally, you can choose to think negatively about others, or you can choose to think compassionately.

A mindfulness practice can be incorporated into many daily activities to make good use of your time. You can practice mindfulness in the shower, while eating, running, driving, doing housework. The list is endless really. Good mindfulness practice does not necessarily need additional time once you have learned how to complete the exercises.

Parks Inner Child Therapy

One of the most effective therapies that I have come across for de-stabilising maladaptive beliefs is Parks Inner Child Therapy or PICT. For some people their belief systems are so rigid and entrenched that CBT is not powerful enough on its own to create flexibility in belief systems. Developed by Penny Parks, a survivor of sexual abuse, PICT works quickly to change belief patterns which in turn helps to make rules more flexible. PICT exercises have the power to reduce the impact of a) vicarious trauma and b) unhelpful maladaptive processes learnt from parents. Changes appear to mainly occur outside of conscious awareness. PICT has yet to be researched fully at a scientific level, although small scale scientific studies have found very powerful effects with individuals who are depressed.

I had my own PICT therapy, and I completed a year's training in it to reach diploma level. I found that the exercises used had the ability to create personal change rapidly. After completing PICT exercises my beliefs did not seem as believable as before and it was a lot easier to stand back from my beliefs and to change my behaviour. PICT is quite dependent on therapeutic input, and although PICT trainers recommend that clients use PICT exercises on their own outside of therapy, in practice it is very difficult due to the high levels of concentration required. This is one of the major drawbacks of PICT. When I have offered PICT by itself to clients I have found that it does not have the longevity of change associated with therapies such as CBT and Mindfulness, where clients can practice a lot of the exercises on their own. On the other hand, I have also found that when PICT is combined with CBT approaches, belief change can be sustained for far longer periods. I will describe one of the more straightforward exercises from PICT (the future most developed self) for you below.

The future most developed self (FMDS) exercise

The FMDS exercise is designed to help you focus on the person that you intend to become someday. It is a self in the future, a person that you will become when you have made all of the changes that you feel that you need to make. A person who is in choice about how he or she lives his/her daily life. This self has all of the necessary inner resources (e.g., compassion, kindness etc) and coping strategies to make the most of his or her life.

The best place to start when using this exercise is to select a problem that you have experienced just lately. This will be a problem involving at least one other person. It will be a problem that you feel you have not handled very well and even now when you think about it, you will be unsure how you could have handled things differently. Run that problem through in your mind and assess how you dealt with it and think about how you felt afterwards. Now scan your body and notice the various uncomfortable feelings that you are experiencing.

To complete the following exercise do whatever you need to do to keep the image of your FMDS in mind. Think about the way she/he looks, thinks, feels and behaves. Once you have completed the construction of your FMDS image step inside your FMDS and watch from inside your FMDS as he/she resolves your problem for you on your behalf. Bear in mind that when your FMDS is solving your problem for you, your everyday-self (i.e., the self inside your FMDS) will be a passive observer and will not do or say anything. The everyday self will simply be watching, listening and feeling how the FMDS feels and noticing what the FMDS does.

Once your FMDS has resolved your problem step outside of your FMDS and assess how your FMDS may have reacted to your problem differently.

Eye Movement Desensitisation & Reprocessing (EMDR)

EMDR is best known for its use with individuals with Post-Traumatic Stress Disorder (PTSD). Rapid eye movement is used in conjunction with accessing traumas, which allows people to process partially processed or unprocessed memories. As unprocessed memories are stored in sub-cortical regions of the brain there is a tendency for many individuals to become emotionally distressed in environments that have cues connected to previous memories. When this occurs people can feel emotionally distressed, but will often not understand why they are feeling the way that they are.

In my experience of having EMDR I was surprised at how effective it was. I went onto the training for it not understanding how it might work and feeling highly sceptical. I was pleasantly surprised at how quickly the process worked and how effective it was. After working on a number of childhood memories I felt more at ease generally. It was as if my anxiety levels had been turned down a notch or two. I had already worked on the same memories previously using person-centred therapy, psychodynamic therapy, neurolinguistics programming, CBT and PICT. EMDR had the most powerful effect on these memories, taking away all the painful emotion connected to them. I felt calmer and relaxed afterwards and the effects were sustained permanently.

Chapter summary

Other therapies for panic attacks

- Many other therapies can also reduce panic symptoms.

- A combination of CBT and medication can work very effectively.

- Mindfulness can be useful to detach from worrying and rumination.

- EMDR can be very useful for working on trauma, and can reduce panic attacks if panic attacks result from past traumatic experiences.

Conclusion

You have now come to the end of this CBT book for panic attacks. In this book we have covered some of the main areas that are covered in CBT sessions for panic attacks. If you decide to attend CBT sessions at some point, hopefully you will have some idea of the types of things that will be discussed.

If you decide to see a CBT therapist your therapist will ask you about what problems in particular you would like to work on. Picking a particular problem and writing down your thoughts and feelings about this problem will be very helpful, as you and your therapist will then be able to discuss it. You may also note down situations that lead to you feeling distressed, and how you think, feel, and behave in these situations. If you are not sure what your main problems are you can complete our online questionnaire. This will give you an idea where you and your therapist might best focus your therapy. I have placed a link below.

http://www.z1b6.com/7.html

You may also need to be aware before you start your CBT that it will involve you changing a) the way that you think, b) how you relate to your feelings and c) how you behave. Changing the way that you think, feel and behave can be very difficult, due to habitual behaviour.

Much of the time we can find ourselves falling into repetitive loops or **habitual behaviours** when we become highly emotional. Many of us use the same habitual behaviours over and over again to deal with our emotions in certain situations, even when we know that our strategies don't work. As I mentioned earlier traditional neuroscience suggests that the seat of habit formation can be found in the basal ganglia, a sub-cortical region of the brain. When we become distressed, states of high emotional arousal lead to primitive brain areas located in the sub-cortical area taking a central role. These primitive brain areas are governed by habitual behaviour, which tends to be automatic, inflexible, and rule-based.

Habitual behaviour is generally thought to operate outside of conscious awareness and we revert to this quite strongly when under stress. I have placed a link below to a video about the basal ganglia, if you want to find out more about it.

http://www.z1b6.com/6.html

CBT can bring your habitual behaviour to your awareness so that you can choose to do things differently. Breaking habitual cycles is not very easy because they are neurologically wired in. However, with repetition, your new positive habits can be stored in your basal ganglia alongside your old habits.

...Very best of luck with your therapy...

Appendix

Regulatory organisations in the UK

British Association of Cognitive and Behavioural Psychotherapists
Imperial House
Hornby Street
Bury
Lancashire
BL9 5BN
Tel: 0161 705 4304   Fax: 0161 705 4306
Email: babcp@babcp.com

British Association for Counselling & Psychotherapy
BACP House
15 St John's Business Park
Lutterworth
LE17 4HB
Tel 01455 883300

British Psychological Society
St Andrews House
48 Princess Road East
Leicester
LE1 7DR
United Kingdom
Tel: +44 (0)116 254 9568
Fax: +44 (0)116 227 1314
Email: **enquiries@bps.org.uk**

Health & Care Professional Council
Park House
184 Kennington Park Road,
London
SE11 4BU,
0300 500 6184

References and additional reading

Arnsten, A, Raskind, M. Taylor, F, & Connor, D. *Neurobiology of Stress (*2015). The effects of stress exposure on prefrontal cortex: Translating basic research into successful treatments for post-traumatic stress disorder, pages 89–99

Bandura, A., (1977). *Social Learning Theory*. Prentice-Hall.

Beck, J. (2011) *Cognitive Behavior Therapy: Second Edition – Basics and Beyond*. The Guildford Press.

Butler, G., (2009). *Overcoming Social Anxiety & Shyness*. Robinson

Cabral, R & Nardi E . *(2012)*. Anxiety and inhibition of panic attacks within translational and prospective research contexts. *Trends in Psychiatry*

Clark, D.M., (1986) A cognitive approach to panic: *Behaviour Research and Therapy*, 24: 461-470

Clark, D.M., & Wells, A (1995). A cognitive model of social phobia. In *Social Phobia – Diagnosis, Assessment, and Treatment* (eds R. G. Heimberg, M. R. Liebowitz, D. Hope, et al), pp. 69–93. New York: Guilford.
Debiec J., & Sullivan, R. (2014). Intergenerational transmission of emotional trauma through amygdala-dependent mother-to-infant transfer of specific fear. *PNAS*, DOI: 10.1073/pnas.1316740111

Golman, D., (1996) .Emotional intelligence: Why it can matter more than IQ. Bloomsbury

Guzmán, Y., Tronson, N., Jovasevic, K., Sato, K., Guedea, A., Mizukami, H., Nishimori, K., & Radulovic. J. (2013) Fear-enhancing effects of septal oxytocin receptors. *Nature Neuroscience*, 2013; DOI: 10.1038/nn.3465

Greenberger, D., & Padesky, C. (1995). *Mind Over Mood: Change How You Feel by Changing the Way That You Think*. Guildford Press Kennerley, H., (2009).

Kennerley, H., (2009). *Overcoming anxiety: A self-help guide using cognitive behavioural techniques*. Robinson

Kinman, G & Grant, L. (2010). Exploring Stress Resilience in Trainee Social Workers: The Role of Emotional and Social Competencies. *British Journal of Social Work*. 10.1093/bjsw/bcq088

Krusemark, E & Li. W., (2012). Enhanced Olfactory Sensory Perception of Threat in Anxiety: An Event-Related fMRI Study (2012). *Chemosensory Perception*, 5 (1): 37 DOI: 10.1007/s12078-011-9111-7

LeDoux JE[1], Iwata J, Cicchetti P, Reis DJ. Different projections of the central amygdaloid nucleus mediate autonomic and behavioral correlates of conditioned fear (1988). *J Neurosci.* Jul;8(7):2517-29.

Logue, M.W., Bauver, S.R., Kremen, W.S., Franz, C.E., Eisen, S.A., Tsuang, M.T., Grant, MD., & Lyons, M.J., (2011). Evidence of Overlapping Genetic Diathesis of Panic Attacks and Gastrointestinal Disorders in a Sample of Male Twin (2011).*Twin Res Hum Gene*t. Feb; 14(1): 16–24. doi: 10.1375/twin.14.1.16

McIlrath, D & Huitt, W. The teaching-learning process: A discussion of models. *Educational Psychology Interactive*. Valdosta, GA: Valdosta State University. Retrieved 2016 from http://www.edpsycinteractive.org/papers/modeltch.html

Moorey S[1] (2010). The six cycles maintenance model: Growing a "vicious flower" for depression. Behaviour and Cognitive Psychotherapy. Mar;38(2):173-84.

Moulding, Richard, Coles, Meredith E., Abramowitz, Jonathan S., Alcolado,Gillian M., Alonso, Pino, Belloch, Amparo, Bouvard, Martine, Clark, David A., Doron, Guy, Fernández-Álvarez, Hector, García-Soriano, Gemma, Ghisi, Marta, Gómez, Beatriz, Inozu, Mujgan, Radomsky, Adam S., Shams, Giti, Sica, Claudio, Simos, Gregoris & Wong, Wing (2014). Part 2. They scare because we care: the relationship between obsessive intrusive thoughts and appraisals and control strategies across 15 cities., *Journal of obsessive-compulsive and related disorders*, vol. 3, no. 3, pp. 280-291.

Rachman, S., Coughtrey, Shafran, R & Radomsky, A., (2015). *The Oxford Guide to the Treatment of Mental Contamination.* The Oxford University Press.

Seger, C.A., (2011). A critical review of habit learning and the Basal ganglia. *Front Syst Neuroscience*, Aug 30;5:66.

Teachman, B., Marker, C & Clerkin, E. (2010). Catastrophic misinterpretations as a predictor of symptom change during treatment for panic disorder (2010). *Consult Clin Psychol*. 78(6): 964–973.

Veale, D., & Wilson, R., (2005). *Overcoming Obsessive Compulsive Disorder: A self-help guide using Cognitive Behavioral Techniques.*. Constable & Robinson Ltd

Wells, A. (1997) Cognitive Therapy of Anxiety Disorders: A Practice Manual and Conceptual Guide. Wiley.
Wilson, R., & Veale, D. (2009). *Overcoming Health Anxiety.* Robinson

Glossary

Academics - Academics spend a lot of time studying or researching specialist subjects at institutions like universities.

Abdominal breathing – Processing of breathing which involves relaxing the abdomen and taking in air to the bottom of the lungs.

Amygdala – Small area of brain tissue within the limbic system, responsible for activating the body's fight-flight-or-freeze response.

Anxiety – An emotion which is experienced when the body is moving into a prepared state to deal with a potential threat.

Automatic responses – Responses which occur automatically/outside of conscious awareness.

Behavioural strategies – Making an adjustment to your behaviour and monitoring the impact of resulting changes.

Catastrophic misinterpretation – A frightening and exaggerated thought connected to magnification of perceived stimuli.

Catecholamines – Chemical messengers used by cells to communicate with one and other.

Cognitive distortions – Thinking patterns that distort perception of reality.

Cognitive models – Ways of explaining how psychological distress is maintained.

Cognitive interventions – Strategies based on changing mental reactions.

Conditioned response – A response that occurs automatically as a result of repeated actions towards particular stimuli.

Coping strategies – Strategies that have been of some assistance in reducing distress.

Core beliefs – Strongly held beliefs about the self.

Counter-intuitive – Ideas which we would not naturally gravitate towards.

Default response – An automatic response based on previous experiences and past conditioning.

Desensitising - Gradually being able to tolerate a feeling by staying in a situation until the feeling feels more bearable.

Diazepam – A medication often prescribed as a muscle relaxant.

Dissociation – A mental and physical state where an individual feels a loss of connection with his or her body.

Distraction – A process that individuals use to avoid experiencing painful emotions.

Emotional reference point – A mechanism used by babies who look towards caregivers to determine how they might react at an emotional level.

Experiential – A process of experiencing through the senses.

External focus – Placing one's attention onto one's external environment.

Habitual behaviours – Behaviours that we are inclined to do because we have do because we have done them so many times before.

Holistic – Multiple process connected together working in parallel.

Hyperventilation – A process of rapid shallow breathing where an individual breathes out too much carbon dioxide.

Hypothesis – An idea based on scientific theory.

Intrusive thoughts – Thoughts that enter awareness uninvited. These thought are usually accompanied by heightened emotion.

Intrusive thoughts – Thoughts that enter awareness uninvited. These thought are usually accompanied by heightened emotion.

Mindfulness – A process of staying in the present moment, bringing conscious awareness back to the present, and deliberately moving away from thoughts about the past or the future.

Mood regulation – An ability to have some management of one's feelings.

Negative automatic thoughts - Thoughts in the background of the mind that have the potential to keep individuals emotionally distressed.

Negative reinforcement – A process of repeated behaviour in which negative emotion is reduced leading to greater likelihood of the same future behaviour.

Neo-cortex – Highly developed area of the mind responsible for logical, rational and analytical thinking. Phobic response – An automatic response associated with heightened anxiety, connected to a specific trigger or cue.

Plasticity – The brains ability to repair itself and grow the more that it is used.

Prefrontal cortex – An area of the brain that acts as a relay between the subcortical regions of the brain and the neo-cortex. It is also responsible for dampening emotional reactions and quietening the mind.

Registered therapists – Registered therapists are members of professional bodies. Professional bodies are organisations that check out their therapists to make sure that they have the required training to do their jobs properly.

Rumination – A cognitive process which involves churning of thoughts connected to the self in the past over and over in the mind.

Safety behaviours - Behaviours utilised to reduce emotional distress in the short-term.

Self-fulfilling prophesy – When something occurs despite your very best attempts to prevent that particular thing occurring.

Self-perpetuating – A situation that is kept in place through its own actions.

Serotonin - A chemical messenger serotine plays a huge part in the body's overall physical and mental Functioning.

Subcortical regions – Brain areas located in the lower half of the brain.

Supressing emotions – An act of pushing down painful or upsetting feelings.

Threat Perception Centre – An area within the brain responsible to

Supressing emotions – An act of pushing down painful or upsetting feelings.

Threat Perception Centre – An area within the brain responsible to noticing stimuli associated with past fear or trauma.

Traumatic incidents – Events that have occurred in the past connected to highly distressing emotions.

Unprocessed memory - An experience that the mind has not fully dealt with.

Vicarious trauma - When people develop trauma responses as a result of observing other people's intense emotional reactions.

Common medications

Alprazolam – A benzodiazepine prescribed for panic, generalised anxiety, phobias, social anxiety, OCD

Amitriptyline – A tricyclic antidepressant

Atenolol – A beta-blocker prescribed for anxiety

Buspirone – A mild tranquiliser prescribed for generalised anxiety, OCD and panic

Chlordiazepoxide – A benzodiazepine prescribed for generalised anxiety, phobias

Citalopram – A selective serotonin reuptake inhibitor commonly prescribed for mixed anxiety and depression

Clomipramine – A tricyclic antidepressant

Clonazepam – A benzodiazepine prescribed for panic, generalised anxiety, phobias, social anxiety

Desipramine – A tricyclic anti-depressant

Diazepam – A benzodiazepine prescribed for generalised anxiety, panic, phobias

Doxepin – A tricyclic antidepressant

Duloxetine – A serotonin-norepinephrine reuptake inhibitor

Escitalopram Oxalate – A selective serotonin reuptake inhibitor

Fluoxetine - A selective serotonin reuptake inhibitor

Fluvoxamine – A selective serotonin reuptake inhibitor

Gabapentin – An anticonvulsant prescribed for generalised anxiety and social anxiety

Imipramine – A tri-cyclic antidepressant

Lorazepam – A benzodiazepine prescribed for generalised anxiety, panic, phobias

Nortriptyline – A tricyclic antidepressant

Oxazepam – A benzodiazepine prescribed for generalised anxiety, phobias

Paroxetine – A selective serotonin reuptake inhibitor

Phenelzine – A monoamine oxidase inhibitor

Pregabalin – An anticonvulsant prescribed for generalised anxiety disorder

Propanalol – A beta blocker prescribed for anxiety

Sertraline - A selective serotonin reuptake inhibitor

Tranylcypromine – A monoamine oxidase inhibitor

Valproate – An anti-convulsant prescribed for panic

Venlafaxine – A serotonin-norepinephrine reuptake inhibitor

Index

Made in the USA
Charleston, SC
11 October 2016